Basic Accounting
for Credit and
Savings Schemes

Nicola Elliott

Oxfam (UK and Ireland)

Published by Oxfam (UK and Ireland)

© Oxfam (UK and Ireland) 1996

ISBN 0 85598 342 6

A catologue record for this book is available from the British Library.

Cover photos: *left:* Linda Milller; *top right:* Jeremy Hartley; *bottom right:* Clare Hanton-Khan
Published by Oxfam (UK and Ireland), 274 Banbury Road, Oxford OX2 7DZ, UK; tel. (0)1865 313922; e-mail publish@oxfam.org.uk

(registered as a charity, no. 202918)

Available from the following agents:
for Canada and the USA: Humanities Press International, 165 First Avenue, Atlantic Highlands, New Jersey NJ 07716-1289, USA; tel. (908) 872 1441; fax (908) 872 0717
for southern Africa: David Philip Publishers, PO Box 23408, Claremont, Cape Town 7735, South Africa; tel. (021) 64 4136; fax (021) 64 3358.

Available in Ireland from Oxfam in Ireland, 19 Clanwilliam Terrace, Dublin 2 (tel. 01 661 8544).

Designed by Oxfam Design Department OX211/PK/96
Printed by Oxfam Print Unit

Oxfam (UK and Ireland) is a member of Oxfam International.

CONTENTS

List of text figures

ACKNOWLEDGEMENTS

The material in this guide is drawn from the ideas presented at a workshop held in Mwanza, Tanzania in December 1993. The participants were members of Youth Economic Groups and Women's Economic Groups supported by Oxfam. The workshop was held to discuss the financial management of revolving loan funds.

I would like to thank John Cammack, Hugh Belshaw, Ros Avery, Susan Ralphs, Ceri Sullivan, and Akm Golam Morshed, who read the manuscript and made helpful suggestions.

Nicola Elliott
May 1996

The view of a well established Estate in a man's bookes procureth contentment unto the possessor.
Richard Dafforne (1635)
The Merchants Mirrour:
or Directions for the Perfect Ordering and Keeping of his Accounts

OMAFES urban credit project, Mali. Maimouna Coulibaly (left) and Fani (right) repaying the weekly instalment of their loan to the collector or 'animatrice' for the loan scheme.   *Photo: James Hawkins/Oxfam*

INTRODUCTION

In many developing countries poor people have combined together to organise saving schemes in order to increase their financial security. Saving schemes may be used as a source of credit for the participants, who take turns to receive loans.

Many donor agencies fund credit schemes in developing countries. Donors are attracted by the idea that their funds will be used many times over and benefit many different borrowers.

There are a range of views on the usefulness and appropriateness of savings and credit schemes (see Further Reading). Much depends on the aim of the scheme. If poverty reduction is the goal, the scheme will need to ensure it responds to the savings and credit needs of very poor people. These may be more to do with flexible savings accounts and provision of loans to meet abnormal expenditure (such as payment for health care or other family expenses) than for credit to set up small income-generating ventures.

Much also depends on the context, including existing formal and informal savings and credit institutions such as banks, rotating savings and credit associations (ROSCAs), and private money-lenders. It is important for intervention agencies to understand how existing institutions are (or are not) useful to poor people and to design any scheme accordingly. The macroeconomic context is important in influencing the financial sustainability of schemes (see Chapter 8: Sustainability). However, institutional sustainability depends on how well staff and people using the scheme work together towards common goals.

Efficient administration and accurate accounting records are vital for any scheme to be successful. A savings and credit scheme needs accurate accounts in order to:

- record the history of the financial activities of the scheme;
- provide information for the leaders of the project to help them to manage its activities;
- maintain confidence in the scheme: donors and savers need to know that their funds are in safe hands; borrowers need to know that their loan is being dealt with fairly.

Accounting is the process of recording, reconciling, sorting, and summarising individual transactions in order to present a picture of the financial health of an enterprise. The purpose of this guide is to explain the principles and tasks required to carry out all these activities for a savings and credit scheme. In many countries there will be a government requirement for organisations to maintain proper accounting records.

It is hoped that the guide will be useful to a number of audiences:

- leaders and finance officers of credit and savings schemes, as the basis for a procedures manual;
- project funders, to provide a benchmark for good practice;
- facilitators of financial training workshops, as a training resource;
- the general reader, as an introduction to basic accounting.

Chapter 1: Getting started

Roles and responsibilities

It is the responsibility of the **management committee** of the project to ensure that its finances are well managed. The committee should elect one committee member to oversee the financial management of the project. This person is usually known as the **treasurer**. The treasurer should be someone with knowledge and experience of financial management.

If the project is a large or complicated one with many transactions there may be too much work for the treasurer who is often a volunteer. It is likely that the project will need to appoint a **bookkeeper** to maintain the accounting records. In some cases it may also be necessary to employ a **cashier** to handle the cash coming in and going out. In smaller organisations the job of bookkeeper and cashier will be done by the same person.

It is good practice to have more than one person working on the accounts of the project, to protect against errors, fraud or suspicion of fraud. Accountants call this **division of duties**. Division of duties protects against fraud because the financial staff would have to act together in order to steal from the project.

The budget

Before *any* expenditure takes place the management committee should draw up and approve a **budget** for the project. A budget should always be drawn up for a fixed period of time, for example, one month or one year.

Firstly, the committee will need to calculate the income likely to be received by the scheme. They will need to estimate the level of savings that they think will be deposited, and include any grants which they expect to receive from donors.

Secondly, they will need to decide what has to be spent in order to run the project, for example, on premises, staff, equipment, and transport; and how much all these expenses are likely to be for the period of the budget.

Using this information the committee can then work out the funds that they will have available to make loans. For example, the budget for a credit and savings scheme might be drawn up as follows:

Credit and savings scheme budget: January 19XX

Income

Grant from donor	200,000
Savings deposited	150,000
Total income	350,000
Expenditure	
Administration	10,000
Available for loans	340,000

Figure 1: Example of the budget of a credit and savings scheme

Procedures

The management committee is responsible for setting out a framework of financial procedures designed to control the financial activities of the project, and for ensuring that the finance officers and other staff are aware of their responsibilities. The procedures explained in this guide could be used as a starting point. However, the management committee will need to decide who is responsible for each task.

In particular, the committee will need to decide the procedure for authorising payments. It may decide that all payments need to be authorised in advance by a committee member, in which case the cashier would need to obtain the signature of a committee member on each payment voucher (see figure 7) before making the payment. All loans made by the credit scheme should be authorised by the committee (see Chapter 6). However, the committee could decide that the cashier may make routine payments up to a certain amount without referring to a committee member.

CHAPTER 2:
RECORDING THE TRANSACTIONS

The cash book

The basic accounting record used to record the cash transactions of the organisation as they happen is known as the **cash book**.

Whenever cash leaves the organisation the cashier records the transaction in the cash book as a payment. Similarly, whenever cash is received by the organisation the cashier records it in the cash book as income.

The cashier should record the transactions in the cash book *as soon as they take place*. This helps to ensure that the transactions are recorded accurately, and that they are all included. Bookkeeping is much easier if it is kept up to date. If everything is written down promptly, the book-keeper does not have to worry that he or she might forget to enter something.

If the cash book is completed accurately it serves as a **diary** of the cash transactions of the organisation.

Information recorded in the cash book

The information which should be recorded in the financial records of the scheme depends on the facts which people involved in the scheme are likely to need to know in the future.

For each payment, people will need answers to the questions:

- When?   • Why?
- Who?   • What?

Therefore, for each payment the bookkeeper should record:

- The date the payment was made.
- The name of the person or organisation who received the payment.
- A description of the purpose of the payment (for example, the goods or services purchased).
- The amount paid out.

In a similar way, for every sum of money received by the organisation the bookkeeper should record:

- The date the income was received.
- The name of the person or organisation paying in the income.
- The reason the income was received.
- The amount received.

The cash book is organised into columns to show this information clearly:

Date	Details[1]	Voucher number[2]	Receipts	Payments	Balance

NOTES:
1 The name of the person receiving the payment and a description of the purpose of the payment.
2 See the section on **Invoices and vouchers** later in this chapter.

Figure 2: Layout of a cash book

There is a column for receipts and a column for payments. The **balance** column is used to record the cash remaining with the organisation after each transaction. The balance is worked out by calculating the total income and deducting the total payments.

Balance = Total receipts – Total payments

Figure 3 gives an example of a completed cash book. The cash held by the organisation on 3 January is 129,000. This is made up of the 130,000 withdrawn from the bank on 2 January less the purchase of stationery for 1,000 on 3 January.

Credit Scheme Cash Book

Date	Details	Voucher	Receipts	Payments	Balance
2 Jan	Withdrawn from bank	R1	130,000		130,000
3 Jan	Purchase stationery	1		1,000	129,000
4 Jan	Refreshments for committee meeting	2		500	128,500
10 Jan	Saver 3 deposit	R2	50,000		178,500
15 Jan	Loan to Group A	3		30,000	148,500
25 Jan	Loan to Group B	4		50,000	98,500
28 Jan	Loan to Group C	5		40,000	58,500

NOTES:
1   There is a separate voucher number sequence for receipts (R1, R2...) and for payments (1,2...).
2   Figures 1 – 48 form a **case study** illustrating the principles explained in Chapters 2 – 8.

Figure 3: Example of a completed cash book

The balance column shows the up-to-date figure of cash available to the organisation.

Another way of laying out a cash book is to show receipts on one page and payments on the opposite page, as shown in figure 4:

Credit Scheme Cash Book

Receipts				Payments			
Date	Description	Voucher	Amount	Date	Description	Voucher	Amount
Jan				Jan			
2	Withdrawn from bank	R1	130,000	3	Purchase stationery	1	1,000
10	Saver 3 deposit	R2	50,000	4	Refreshments for committee meeting	2	500
				15	Loan to Group A	3	30,000
				25	Loan to Group B	4	50,000
				28	Loan to Group C	5	40,000
				31	Closing balance		*58,500*
Total			180,000	Total			180,000

Figure 4: Alternative layout for a cash book

In this system, the balance is not worked out after every transaction. It can be calculated at any time by deducting total payments from total receipts. For example, on 31 January the total receipts in the month were 180,000. Total payments were 121,500. Therefore, the balance was 58,500.

At the end of the month the cashier should calculate the balance remaining (the **closing balance**) and enter it as if it were the last payment of the month. When this is done, the two sides of the cash book add up to the same amount, as shown in figure 4.

The cash balance remaining at the end of the month (the closing balance) becomes the **opening balance** for the start of the following month. The opening balance is entered as if it were the first receipt in the cash book at the start of the month. (See figure 27.)

The cashier should count the actual cash in the cash box and ensure that the amount is the same as the closing balance shown in the cash book. (See Chapter 3: Balancing the Books: The Cash Count.)

Cash handling

The project should purchase a safe in which to keep the cash and important documents. The cash box, cheque book, loan agreements, and unused receipt vouchers should always be stored in the locked safe.

The cashier should keep the cash belonging to the project in a locked **cash box** which should be kept in the locked safe when not in use. Only the **cashier** should have access to the cash box. The same person should be responsible for writing up the cash book.

A member of the management committee should hold the spare key to the cash box. The key should be kept in a sealed envelope. The cashier and the committee member should both sign over the seal, and date the envelope.

This procedure ensures that the management committee can have access to the cash in an emergency but at any time the committee member holding the spare key can prove that she or he has not opened the cash box.

The bank book

In most situations, it is advisable for security reasons for organisations, however small, to have an account at a bank. Many donor organisations will insist on bank accounts for groups they support. The transactions of an organisation with its bank are recorded in the **bank book**.

The **bank book** is exactly the same as the **cash book** except that it records transactions through the bank instead of transactions in cash. (See figure 5.) Sometimes both the bank book and the cash book are referred to as 'the cash book(s)'.

Credit Scheme Bank Book

Date	Description	Cheque no.	Voucher	Receipts	Payments	Balance
Jan						
1	Grant from donor		BR 1	200,000		200,000
2	Saver 1 deposit		BR 2	25,000		225,000
2	Saver 2 deposit		BR 3	45,000		270,000
2	Cash withdrawn	000051	1		130,000	140,000
5	Loan to Group D	000052	2		50,000	90,000
15	Vehicle hire for field visit	000053	3		1,300	88,700
16	Payment of office rent	000054	4		5,000	83,700
28	Loan to Group E	000055	5		45,000	38,700
31	Saver 4 deposit		BR 4	13,000		*51,700*

Figure 5: Example of a completed bank book

As for a cash book, the alternative presentation, with receipts on one page and payments on the opposite page, may be used for the bank book, as shown in figure 6 overleaf.

Payments through the bank are usually made by cheque. The bookkeeper should record the cheque number in the bank book, as shown in figures 5 and 6.

The management committee will need to appoint two or more of its members to sign the cheques. This could be the treasurer and another committee member. The committee will need to decide and to inform the bank whether each signatory can sign alone or whether two signatures are required on each cheque. They may decide that cheques below a certain limit need only one signature and cheques over that limit need two signatures.

The bookkeeper should keep the unused cheques locked in the safe.

Invoices and vouchers

For most transactions it is likely that there will be more information which it would be useful to record than there is room to write in the cash book or bank book.

For example, for payments to suppliers it will be useful to have a record of the exact quantities purchased. In many cases suppliers will provide an

Credit Scheme Bank Book

Receipts				Payments				
Date	Description	BR	Amount	Date	Description	Voucher	Cheque no.	Amount
Jan			Jan	Jan				
1	Grant from donor	1	200,000	2	Cash withdrawn	1	51	130,000
2	Saver 1 deposit	2	25,000	5	Loan to Group D	2	52	50,000
2	Saver 2 deposit	3	45,000	15	Vehicle hire	3	53	1,300
31	Saver 4 deposit	4	13,000	16	Office rent	4	54	5,000
				28	Loan to group E	5	55	45,000
				31	Closing balance			*51,700*
Total			283,000	Total				283,000

Figure 6: Alternative layout for a bank book

invoice, which sets out what is being supplied and the cost of each item. The invoices should be numbered and filed in numerical order, so that they are available to refer to if there is a query about any item in the cash book.

Invoices are an important part of the accounting records because they provide evidence to support the information entered in the cash book. If an invoice is not available, or not appropriate, for a particular payment, a **payment voucher** can be used. Like an invoice, a payment voucher records who has been paid, the amount paid and the purpose of the payment. There should also be a space for the signature of the person authorising the payment and the person receiving the money.

Payment voucher

Credit scheme _____ Voucher number __*000056*__

Paid to ___*Saver 4*___ Amount __*3,000*__

Description __*Repaid by cheque*__

Authorised by _*Cashier*_ Received by __*Saver 4*__ Date __*8 February 19XX*__

Figure 7: Example of a payment voucher

When a cheque payment is required, the bookkeeper should prepare the cheque and present it together with the payment voucher or invoice to the relevant committee member(s) for signing. (This is an example of the **division of duties** principle referred to in Chapter 1.)

Whenever money is received by the organisation the cashier should issue a **receipt voucher**. The cashier should retain copies of the receipt vouchers and file them in numerical order.

Receipt voucher

Credit scheme _____ Voucher number _*R7*_

Received from ____*Saver 3*____ Amount __*500*__

Description ____*Deposit*____

Received by __*Cashier*__ Date __*25 February 19XX*__

Figure 8: Example of a receipt voucher

The cash book should have a column in which to enter voucher numbers. There should be a separate number series for receipts and payments. For example, in figure 3, the payment voucher sequence starts with '1' and the receipt voucher sequence starts with 'R1'.

Receipt vouchers are particularly important for a credit and savings scheme: when retained by participants they provide evidence of loan repayments made and savings deposited.

The project should purchase books of receipt vouchers which are pre-numbered. It is then easy to check that all of them are accounted for properly in the cash book. If pre-numbered books are not available, the treasurer should hand-write numbers on the receipts in the receipt book before issuing them to the bookkeeper. Unused receipt vouchers should be locked away, to ensure that only genuine receipts are issued.

A summary of this chapter

1 The basic accounting record of any organisation or project is the **cash book**. If the project has a bank account it will also need a **bank book**.
2 The bookkeeper should always keep the cash and bank books up to date. She or he should enter transactions in the cash or bank book *as soon as* money is received or a payment is made.
3 Only one person should have access to the cash box.
4 The bookkeeper should make sure that there is an **invoice** or **payment voucher** for every payment made.
5 The bookkeeper should issue a **receipt voucher** for all income received.

Chapter 3: Balancing the books

The cash count

Chapter 2 explained that, if the cash book is written up accurately, the balance column shows the cash held by the organisation at any point in time.

In order to ensure that the accounting records reflect the true situation, there should be a regular check that the amount of cash in the organisation's cash box or safe is actually the same as the amount shown in the cash book. The cashier should count the cash and compare the total with the cash book balance.

It is useful to record the cash count so that if a difference arises in the future there is a record of the last time the cash book and the cash box agreed. (See figure 9.)

Cash count at 31 January 19XX	
Cash counted	
Notes:	
1000 x 50	50,000
500 x 16	8,000
100 x 5	500
Coins:	———
Total cash counted on 31 January 19XX:	58,500
Cash book balance on 31 January 19XX:	58,500
Difference (if any):	NIL
Counted by: (cashier) _____	Date: 31 January 19XX
Agreed by: (treasurer) _____	Date: 31 January 19XX

Figure 9: A cash count record sheet

The treasurer should review the cash count and initial the cash count sheet. *A cash count should be carried out and recorded at least once each month (on the last day of the month) and whenever responsibility for the cash box is handed over to another person.*

The bank statement

The bank will issue a monthly statement of its transactions on behalf of the project. The statement will probably look similar to the bank book, with separate columns for the date of the transaction, the type of transaction, and the amounts. (See figure 10.)

Bank Statement: January 19XX		Withdrawals	Deposits	Balance
2 Jan	Deposit		70,000	70,000
2 Jan	Deposit		200,000	270,000
2 Jan	Cheque 000051	130,000		140,000
18 Jan	Cheque 000054	5,000		135,000
18 Jan	Cheque 000052	50,000		85,000
19 Jan	Cheque 000053	1,300		83,700
31 Jan	Charges	1,000		82,700

NOTE: The deposits on January 2 from Saver 1 (25,000) and Saver 2 (45,000) are shown as one amount of 70,000 on the bank statement; the example assumes that they were paid into the bank at the same time.

Figure 10: An example of a bank statement

The bank statement is the bank's record of the project's transactions through the bank. Therefore, the transactions shown should match *exactly* with those shown in the bank book. The bookkeeper should investigate anything which does not match exactly in case there is an error in the bank book or at the bank.

There may, however, be differences between the bank statement and the bank book due to differences in *timing*. When the project issues a cheque to a supplier or to a participant in the credit scheme the bookkeeper should enter the details of the cheque in the bank book immediately. Even if the person receiving the cheque deposits it at their bank on the same day, it will take a few days for the cheque to work its way through the banking system and to appear on the project's statement. Cheques issued towards the end of the month may not appear on the bank statement for that month: but they should appear on the following month's statement.

The bank reconciliation

In order to check that the bank statement agrees with the bank book the bookkeeper should prepare a **bank reconciliation**. A bank reconciliation is an explanation of the difference, if any, between the balance shown in the bank book and the balance shown on the bank statement.

The bookkeeper should go through the bank statement item by item and find the matching item in the bank book. She or he should mark the matching items in the bank book and on the statement with a tick, as shown in figures 11 and 12.

Date	Description	Cheque no.	Voucher	Receipts	Payments	Balance
Jan						
1	Grant from donor		BR 1	200,000 ✓		200,000
2	Saver 1 deposit		BR 2	25,000 ✓		225,000
2	Saver 2 deposit		BR 3	45,000 ✓		270,000
2	Cash withdrawn	000051	1		130,000 ✓	140,000
5	Loan to Group D	000052	2		50,000 ✓	90,000
15	Vehicle hire for field visit	000053	3		1,300 ✓	88,700
16	Payment of office rent	000054	4		5,000 ✓	83,700
28	Loan to Group E	000055	5		45,000	38,700
31	Saver 4 deposit		BR 4	13,000		51,700

Credit Scheme Bank Book

Figure 11: Bank book: to show reconciliation with bank statement

		Withdrawals	Deposits	Balance
2 Jan	Deposit		70,000 ✓	70,000
2 Jan	Deposit		200,000 ✓	270,000
2 Jan	Cheque 000051	130,000 ✓		140,000
18 Jan	Cheque 000054	5,000 ✓		135,000
18 Jan	Cheque 000052	50,000 ✓		85,000
19 Jan	Cheque 000053	1,300 ✓		83,700
31 Jan	Charges	1,000		82,700

Bank Statement: January 19XX

Figure 12: Bank statement: to show reconciliation with bank book

When this exercise is complete there may be some items not ticked. When these are listed, they should explain any difference between the bank book balance and the statement balance.

In our example, there is an unticked item on the bank statement (the charges of 1,000) and two unticked items in the bank book (cheque no. 000054 for 45,000 and the deposit of 13,000 on 31 January). We can list these as follows:

Bank reconciliation at 31 January 19XX

Balance on bank statement	82,700
Less:	
Payment in bank book not on statement	
Cheque 000055	(45,000)
	37,700
Add:	
Income in bank book not on statement	
Deposit on 31 January	13,000
Payments on statement not yet in bank book	
Charges	1,000
Balance shown in bank book	51,700

Prepared by: (bookkeeper)	Date: 31 January 19XX
Agreed by: (treasurer)	Date: 31 January 19XX

NOTE: It is a convention in accounting to show payments in brackets, if both receipts and payments appear in the same column, in order to distinguish between them.

Figure 13: Example of a bank reconciliation

The bank reconciliation in this example shows that the difference between the balance in the bank book at 31 January (51,700) and the balance on the bank statement (82,700) is due to timing differences:

- Cheque number 000055 for 45,000 was issued on 28 January as a loan to Group E but had not appeared on the bank statement by 31 January. It should appear on the statement for February. If it does not appear in February the project should contact Group E to find out why they have not presented the cheque at their bank.

- A charge of 1,000 has been made by the bank for administering the account. This does not yet appear in the bank book because the project did not know how much the charge would be until they received the statement. The charge should be entered in the bank book for February.
- The 13,000 deposited on 31 January has not yet been recorded by the bank in the project's account. The bookkeeper should check that it appears on the February statement.

Once the **cash count** has been checked against the cash book and the **bank statement** has been reconciled with the bank book, we can say that the accounts for the month have been **balanced**.

A summary of this chapter

1 The bookkeeper should **balance** the accounts each month by counting the cash and reconciling the bank book balance to the bank statement.
2 The treasurer should review and initial the cash count and the bank reconciliation.
3 A cash count should be carried out whenever responsibility for the cash box is handed over to another person.

Chapter 4: Sorting the data

Accounts are not an end in themselves. They are designed to provide information to those who have an interest in the project: the donors, savers, and borrowers.

The columns of figures in the cash and bank books provide a day by day historical record of the financial activities of the project, rather than a summary of its financial position. The cash books provide the *data from which the financial position can be calculated*. The bookkeeper needs to sort and summarise that data in order to provide useful *information* for the managers of the project. **Management information** is the term used by accountants to describe financial summaries prepared for managers.

Initially the transactions are sorted into payments and receipts. In order to provide more information, the items can be further sorted into categories. These categories should match the categories in the budget.

In a credit and savings scheme the main categories of income are likely to be:

- grants received from donors
- loan interest
- loan repayments
- savings deposited.

In order to sort the income into these categories the bookkeeper needs to include a column in the cash book for each category. There should also be an 'other' column to record items which do not fall into any of the budgeted categories. Accountants call this type of cash book an **analysed cash book** because it sorts or *analyses* the transactions into the selected categories. Figure 14 gives an example.

Credit scheme cash book

Receipts

Date	Description	Voucher	Amount	Grants	Loans repaid	Loan interest	Savings	Other
2 Jan	Withdrawn from bank	R1	130,000					130,000
10 Jan	Saver 3 deposit	R2	50,000				50,000	
Total			180,000				50,000	130,000

Figure 14: Analysed cash book: receipts

In an analysed cash book each transaction is entered twice: once in the amount column and again in the appropriate category column.

For example, in figure 14, the withdrawal of 130,000 from the bank on 2 January appears in the 'amount' column *and* in the column for the category 'other'; the deposit from Saver 3 on 10 January appears in the 'amount' column *and* in the column for the category 'savings'.

At the end of the month the column totals will show the total income received in each category during the month. In order to ensure that the analysed cash book 'balances', the bookkeeper should check that the analysis column totals add up to the total of the 'amount' column. For example, in figure 14, the total of the 'savings' column (50,000) plus the total of the 'other' column (130,000) add up to the total of the 'amount' column (180,000).

The budgeted categories of payments for a credit and saving scheme are likely to be:

- loans issued
- administration expenses
- savings paid back to participants.

Therefore, the bookkeeper could set up the payments side of the cash book to look like figure 15:

Credit scheme cash book

Payments Date	Description	Voucher	Amount	Loans issued	Savings repaid	Administration expenses	Other
3 Jan	Purchase stationery	1	1,000			1,000	
4 Jan	Refreshments	2	500			500	
15 Jan	Loan to group A	3	30,000	30,000			
25 Jan	Loan to group B	4	50,000	50,000			
28 Jan	Loan to group C	5	40,000	40,000			
31 Jan	Closing balance		58,500				58,500
Total			180,000	120,000		1,500	58,500

Figure 15: Analysed cash book: payments

The receipts and payments report

Using the column totals from the analysed cash book, the bookkeeper can summarise the cash transactions of the project for the month of January as follows:

Credit scheme cash book
Receipts and payments summary January 19XX

Opening balance	NIL
Receipts	
Cash from bank	130,000
Savings deposited	50,000
	180,000
Payments	
Administration	(1,500)
Loans issued	(120,000)
Closing balance	58,500

Figure 16: Receipts and payments summary from cash book

The bookkeeper should sort the receipts and payments in the bank book in the same way as for the cash book. This is shown in figures 17 and 18.

Credit scheme bank book
Receipts

Date	Description	Voucher	Amount	Grants	Loans repaid	Loan interest	Savings	Other
1 Jan	Grant from donor	BR1	200,000	200,000				
2 Jan	Saver 1 deposit	BR2	25,000				25,000	
2 Jan	Saver 2 deposit	BR3	45,000				45,000	
31 Jan	Saver 4 deposit	BR4	13,000				13,000	
Total			283,000	200,000			83,000	

Figure 17: Analysed bank book: receipts

Credit scheme bank book

Payments

Date	Description	Cheque	Voucher	Amount	Loans issued	Savings repaid	Admin expenses	Other
2 Jan	Cash withdrawn	000051	1	130,000				130,000
5 Jan	Loan to group D	000052	2	50,000	50,000			
15 Jan	Vehicle hire	000053	3	1,300			1,300	
16 Jan	Office rent	000054	4	5,000			5,000	
28 Jan	Loan to group E	000055	5	45,000	45,000			
31 Jan	Closing balance			*51,700*				*51,700*
Total				283,000	95,000		6,300	181,700

Figure 18: Analysed bank book: payments

Using the analysed bank book, the bookkeeper can summarise the bank transactions for the month of January:

Credit scheme bank book
Receipts and payments summary January 19XX

Opening balance	NIL
Receipts	
Grant from donor	200,000
Savings deposited	<u>83,000</u>
	283,000
Payments	
To cash	(130,000)
Administration	(6,300)
Loans issued	<u>(95,000)</u>
Closing balance	<u>51,700</u>

Figure 19: Receipts and payments summary from bank book

The bookkeeper can then combine these two summaries to provide a complete report of the project's transactions for the month. Accountants call this a **receipts and payments report**.

Receipts and Payments Report: January 19XX

Opening balance	NIL
Receipts	
Grant from donor	200,000
Savings deposited (50,000 + 83,000)	<u>133,000</u>
	333,000
Payments	
Administration (1,500 + 6,300)	(7,800)
Loans issued (120,000 + 95,000)	<u>(215,000)</u>
Closing balance (58,500 + 51,700)	<u>(110,200)</u>

NOTE: The withdrawal of cash (130,000 shown as a receipt in the cash book and as a payment in the bank book) does not appear on this combined statement because it is not a transaction with the outside world: it is simply a transfer of the project's money from the bank into the cash safe.

Figure 20: Example of a receipts and payments report

The example above in figure 20 is the receipts and payments report for the month of January. A receipts and payments report can be prepared for any length of time. Accountants call the length of time covered by a report the **accounting period**.

The budget and actual report

The bookkeeper can combine the receipts and payments report with the budget to produce a **budget and actual report**:

Budget and Actual Report: January 19XX

	Budget	Actual	Variance
Income			
Grant from donor	200,000	200,000	0
Savings deposited	150,000	133,000	17,000
Expenditure			
Administration	10,000	7,800	2,200
Loans issued	340,000	215,000	125,000

Figure 21: Example of a budget and actual report

The **variance** column shows the difference between the budgeted amounts of income and expenditure and the actual amounts.

The committee should review the budget and actual report each month in order to monitor the financial progress of the scheme. For example, in figure 21 the variance column shows that savings deposited, administration expenses, and loans issued were all less than budgeted.

A summary of this chapter

1 In order to provide **management information** the bookkeeper needs to sort and summarise the individual transactions (the data) of the project.
2 The bookkeeper can sort the transactions as they happen by entering them in the columns of an **analysed cash book**. There should be a column heading for each budgeted category of income and expenditure.
3 Using the information from the analysed cash books, the bookkeeper can prepare monthly summary reports known as the **receipts and payments report** and the **budget and actual report**.
4 The management committee should review the monthly summary reports in order to monitor the financial progress of the scheme.

Chapter 5: The balance sheet

Assets and liabilities

The receipts and payments report introduced in Chapter 4 tells the story of an organisation's financial activities during a particular accounting period.

It shows the cash and bank balances held at the start of the accounting period. It shows the income received and the payments made during the period which resulted in the cash and bank balances remaining at the end of the period.

However, apart from the amount of money held in cash or at the bank, the receipts and payments report does not show *the financial position* at the end of the accounting period. In order to monitor the progress of the credit scheme, the management committee need to keep track of the **assets** and **liabilities** of the project.

The **assets** of an organisation are the things that it *owns*. These include equipment and stock. Monies due to be *paid to* the organisation also count as assets; loans issued and not yet repaid are therefore assets. Those who owe money to the organisation are known as **debtors**.

From the Receipts and Payments Report shown in figure 20, we can list the assets of the credit scheme in the case study at 31 January:

Credit scheme: assets at 31 January 19XX	
Cash held (from figure 16)	58,500
Bank balance (from figure 19)	51,700
Loans issued	215,000
Total assets	325,200

The **liabilities** of an organisation are the amounts it must *pay to* other organisations or individuals. Therefore savings deposited with the project are liabilities of the project. The organisations or individuals which must be paid are known as **creditors**.

For example, if you have money deposited at a bank, the bank is your debtor because the bank must pay your money to you when you request it. However, if you have an overdraft at the bank, the bank is your creditor because you must pay money to the bank to clear the overdraft.

From figure 20, we can list the liabilities of the credit scheme in the case study at 31 January as follows:

Credit scheme: liabilities at 31 January 19XX

Savings deposited	133,000
Total liabilities	133,000

We can combine the list of assets with the list of liabilities to calculate the **net assets** at 31 January 19XX:

Credit scheme: calculation of net assets at 31 January 19XX

Assets		
Cash held	58,500	
Bank balance	51,700	
Loans issued	215,000	
Total assets		325,200
Liabilities		
Savings deposited	133,000	
Total liabilities		133,000
Total assets less total liabilities		192,200
= net assets		

Figure 22: Calculation of net assets

Net assets represent the current value of the project: the money that would be left over if the project used what it *owns* to pay what it *owes*.

Capital

The original funding of a project or organisation is known as the **capital.** In the case study the capital of the credit and savings scheme is the initial grant of 200,000.

The balance sheet

The report which summarises the **assets and liabilities** of an organisation is known as the **balance sheet**. This is drawn up by comparing the net assets of the project with the capital. On 1 January 19XX, the balance sheet of the scheme would have been:

Balance Sheet at 1 January 19XX

Assets		**Capital**	
Bank balance	200,000	Grant received	200,000
Net assets	200,000		200,000

Figure 23: Balance sheet at 1 January

At 31 January the net assets can be listed as follows:

Balance Sheet at 31 January 19XX (extract)

Assets		**Capital**
Cash held	58,500	Grant received 200,000
Bank balance	51,700	
Loans outstanding	215,000	
Liabilities		
Savings held	133,000	
Net assets	192,200	

Figure 24: Extract from balance sheet at 31 January

The difference between the net assets at the start and at the end of an accounting period is the surplus or deficit for that accounting period.

In the case study the net assets at 1 January were 200,000. On 31 January the net assets were 192,200. Therefore, the deficit for January was 200,000 – 192,200 = 7,800. When this figure is inserted into the balance sheet, the two sides add up to the same amount:

Balance Sheet at 31 January 19XX

Assets		Represented by	
Cash held	58,500	Grant received	200,000
Bank balance	51,700	Deficit	(7,800)
Loans outstanding	215,000		
Total assets	325,200		
Liabilities			
Savings held	(133,000)		
Net assets	192,200		192,200

Figure 25: Balance sheet at 31 January

Accountants call this report the balance sheet because the two columns add up to the same figure. If the two sides do not balance, there is a mistake which needs to be investigated and corrected.

The left hand side of the balance sheet lists the assets and liabilities of the project in order to calculate the **net assets** position. This is the amount of money that would remain if the project used its assets to pay off all its creditors.

The right hand side explains *how the project arrived at* its current net assets position. In this example, the project received a grant of 200,000. It has spent 7,800 on administration (see figure 20), leaving net assets of 192,200.

Extending the case study
In order to illustrate the balance sheet concept more clearly we need to continue the case study. We take up the story again in February 19XX.

The budget has been drawn up as follows:

Credit and savings scheme budget February 19XX

Income

Balance brought forward from January	110,200
Loan repayments[1]	17,917
Interest on loans[2]	1,792
Savings deposited[3]	10,000
Total income	139,909

Expenditure

Administration	2,000
Savings repaid[3]	5,000
Loans issued	70,000
Balance carried forward	62,909

NOTES:
1 In the case study, loans are repayable in 12 monthly instalments starting one month after the loan is issued. In January 215,000 was issued in loans (see figure 20), therefore, 215,000 ÷ 12 = 17,917 is due to be repaid in February.
2 Interest is charged on loans at 10 per cent. The interest is payable in 12 monthly instalments starting one month after the loan is issued. Therefore, interest payments due in February are 215,000 x 10% ÷ 12 = 1,792.
3 The figures for savings deposited and repaid are estimates by the management committee of the likely level of savings which will be deposited with and withdrawn from the scheme.

Figure 26: Credit and savings scheme budget for February

In February 19XX the following transactions take place:

1 February	Saver 1 deposits 2,000 in cash.
2 February	Saver 2 deposits 1,500 in cash.
2 February	Group B makes a loan repayment in cash of 4,583 of which 416 is interest.
5 February	Group C makes a loan repayment by cheque of 3,667 of which 334 is interest.
7 February	Saver 3 deposits 3,000 in cash.

8 February	3,000 is paid back to Saver 4 using cheque number 000056.
10 February	Group A makes a loan repayment in cash of 2,750 of which 250 is interest.
15 February	Saver 5 deposits 2,000 in cash.
16 February	500 is paid in cash for the hire of a room for the committee meeting.
16 February	Refreshments for committee meeting: 100 cash.
17 February	20,000 is deposited at the bank.
17 February	Loan issued to Group F: 30,000 using cheque 000057.
25 February	Saver 3 deposits 500 in cash.

The cash and bank books for February are shown in figures 27 to 30. (Readers might like to take the opportunity to practise the procedures covered so far by writing up the February cash and bank books themselves. Blank forms are included in Appendix 3 at the end of the book.)

Credit scheme cash book

Receipts

Date	Description	Voucher	Amount	Grants	Loans repaid	Loan interest	Savings	Other
February								
1	Opening balance		58,500					58,500
1	Saver 1 deposit	R1	2,000				2,000	
2	Saver 2 deposit	R2	1,500				1,500	
2	Group B loan repayment	R3	4,583		4,167	416		
7	Saver 3 deposit	R4	3,000				3,000	
10	Group A loan repayment	R5	2,750		2,500	250		
15	Saver 5 deposit	R6	2,000				2,000	
25	Saver 3 deposit	R7	500				500	
Total			74,833		6,667	666	9,000	58,500

Figure 27: Cash book: receipts (February)

Credit scheme cash book

Payments

Date	Description	Voucher	Amount	Loans issued	Savings repaid	Admin expenses	Other
February							
16	Hire of room	1	500			500	
16	Refreshments	2	100			100	
17	To bank	3	20,000				20,000
28	Closing balance		54,233				54,233
Total			74,833			600	74,233

Figure 28: Cash book: payments (February)

Credit scheme bank book

Receipts

Date	Description	Voucher	Amount	Grants	Loans repaid	Loan interest	Savings	Other
February								
1	Opening balance		51,700					51,700
5	Group C loan repayment	BR1	3,667		3,333	334		
17	From cash	BR2	20,000					20,000
Total			75,367		3,333	334		71,700

NOTE: The loan repayment is split between two of the analysis columns. This is because part of the payment is to repay the loan and part of it is the payment of interest on the loan.

Figure 29: Bank book: receipts (February)

Credit scheme bank book

Payments

Date	Description	Voucher	Amount	Loans issued	Savings repaid	Admin expenses	Other
February							
1	Bank charges		1,000			1,000	
8	To saver 4	000056	3,000		3,000		
17	Group F loan	000057	30,000	30,000			
28	Closing balance		41,367				41,367
Total			75,367	30,000	3,000	1,000	41,367

Figure 30: Bank book: payments (February)

From the analysed cash and bank books for February we can produce the receipts and payments report and the budget and actual report:

Receipts and Payments Report: February 19XX

Opening balance (58,500 + 51,700)	110,200
Receipts	
Loans repaid (3,333 + 6,667)	10,000
Loan interest (334 + 666)	1,000
Savings deposited	9,000
	130,200
Payments	
Loans issued	(30,000)
Savings repaid	(3,000)
Admin expenses (1,000 + 600)	(1,600)
Closing balance (54,233 + 41,367)	95,600

Note: A receipts and payment report is for a period of time (an accounting period) whereas a balance sheet shows the financial position at a chosen date– the last day of the accounting period.

Figure 31: Receipts and payments report (February)

Budget and Actual Report: February 19XX

	Budget	Actual	Variance
Income			
Balance brought forward	110,200	110,200	0
Loan repayments	17,917	10,000	7,917
Interest on loans	1,792	1,000	792
Savings deposited	10,000	9,000	1,000
Expenditure			
Administration	2,000	1,600	400
Savings repaid	5,000	3,000	2,000
Loans issued	70,000	30,000	40,000
Balance carried forward	62,909	95,600	(32,691)

Figure 32: Budget and actual report (February)

From the receipts and payments report in figure 31, we can go on to prepare the balance sheet as 28 February:

Balance Sheet at 28 February 19XX

	Notes	28 February	31 January[1]
Assets			
Cash		54,233	58,500
Bank balance		41,367	51,700
Loans outstanding	1	235,000	215,000
Total Assets		330,600	325,200
Liabilities			
Savings held	2	(139,000)	(133,000)
Net Assets		191,600	192,200
Represented by:			
Grant received		200,000	200,000
Accumulated deficit	3	(8,400)	(7,800)
Net assets		191,600	192,200

Notes on the calculations:

1 Loans outstanding:

Opening loans outstanding	215,000	–
Add: Loans issued	30,000	215,000
Less: Loans repaid (excluding interest)	(10,000)	–
	235,000	215,000

2 Savings held:

Opening savings held	133,000	–
Add: Savings deposited	9,000	133,000
Less: Savings repaid	(3,000)	–
	139,000	133,000

3 Accumulated deficit:

Opening deficit	7,800	–
Add: Administration expenses	1,600	7,800
Less: Interest received	(1,00	–
	8,400	7,800

NOTE: 1 It is useful to show the previous balance sheet for comparison. The example shows a reduction in net assets between 31 January and 28 February from 192,200 to 191,600. The project has spent more on administration than it has earned in interest.

Figure 33: Balance sheet (28 February)

Types of expenditure

The balance sheet in figure 33 shows that the project in the case study spent 1,600 on administration expenses in February. These expenses (bank charges, room hire, refreshments) represented the running costs of the project during February. The project benefited from these expenses *during* February. Accountants call this type of expenditure **revenue expenditure**. Other costs, such as rent, salaries, and fuel, also come into the category of revenue expenditure.

Expenditure on items which will be used during *more than one* accounting period is called **capital expenditure**. Capital expenditure is expenditure on **assets** such as equipment, furniture, or vehicles.

Expenditure on capital items (assets) is not part of the administration expenses of an accounting period: instead, it is shown in the assets section of the balance sheet, together with the cash, bank balance, and stock.

For example, if the project in the case study issues a cheque for 10,000 to purchase office equipment, the balance sheet in figure 33 will be amended as follows:

Balance Sheet at 28 February 19XX		
	28 February	**31 January**
Assets		
Cash	54,233	58,500
Bank balance (41,367 - 10,000)	31,367	51,700
Furniture	10,000	—
Loans outstanding	235,000	215,000
Total Assets	330,600	325,200
Liabilities		
Savings held	(139,000)	(133,000)
Net Assets	191,600	192,200
Represented by:		
Grant received	200,000	200,000
Accumulated deficit	(8,400)	(7,800)
Net assets	191,600	192,200

Figure 34: Balance sheet (28 February) showing capital expenditure

A summary of this chapter

1 In order to monitor the financial health of the project, the project leaders need to review regularly the assets and liabilities of the project as shown on the **balance sheet**.

2 The bookkeeper or treasurer should prepare a balance sheet for each committee meeting.

3 The balance sheet is in two parts: the calculation of net assets and the explanation of how the net assets were acquired.

4 In preparing the balance sheet, a distinction is made between **capital expenditure** (expenditure on **assets** which will be used during several accounting periods) and **revenue expenditure** (expenditure on running costs during a particular accounting period).

Chapter 6:
Administration of loans

Loan applications

The management committee of a credit scheme should consider each loan application carefully. Money should only be lent to people who are likely to be able to repay.

Each application should include a **budget** and a **repayment plan**. The **budget** is a list of the items to be purchased with the loan, and should include an estimate of the cost of each item. The **repayment plan** is a forecast of how the group will generate the money to repay their loan.

Group A: Dressmaking project

Budget:

Sewing machine	25,000
Table and stool	4,000
Threads	1,000
	30,000

(Outfits to be made up using clients' own fabric.)

Repayment plan:

20 outfits per month at 3,000 each	60,000
Monthly repayments from February 19XX	(2,750)
Available for group members	57,250

Figure 35: Example of a project budget

Loan agreements

A loan agreement should be drawn up for every loan advanced by the scheme. This is to ensure that the borrower understands what the loan is for and how it is to be repaid. The loan agreement should set out:

- the amount of the loan;
- the purpose of the loan;

- the interest charge;
- the timing of repayments;
- any penalties for late repayment.

An example is shown in figure 36.

Credit scheme loan agreement

Name of group: ___*Group A*___

The credit scheme has agreed to lend you the sum of ___*30,000.*
Interest on this loan will be charged at the rate of ___*10%*___ per annum.
The credit scheme agrees that the total amount of the loan, plus interest of *3000* will be repaid in 12 monthly instalments of _*2,750,*_ starting on_*15 February 19XX .*

The money lent by the credit scheme must be used only for the agreed purpose, namely, ___*the purchase of a sewing machine, table, stool, and threads*___ .
Interest will be charged on late repayments at the rate of 2% per month.

If any repayment is more than one month late, the credit scheme reserves the right to confiscate _*the sewing machine*___ until a new repayment plan is agreed with the group.

Signed on behalf of the credit scheme:

Name _____ Position _____

Signature _____ Date _____

Signed on behalf of the group:

Name _____ Position _____

Signature _____ Date _____

Figure 36: Example of a loan agreement

When the loan is issued a representative of the group should sign the loan agreement and the payment voucher (see figure 7).

Interest

Borrowers will normally be required to pay back to a credit scheme more than they originally borrowed: there will be an **interest** or **administration charge** added to the loan.

The management committee will need to set the level of interest to be charged (see Chapter 8: Sustainability) and to decide on the method of calculating the loan repayments.

The simplest method of calculating interest is the **straight-line method**. Here, the interest is spread equally over all the repayments. For example, a loan of 30,000 is to be repaid in 12 monthly instalments. There is an administration charge or interest of 10 per cent (3,000). Using the straight-line method, there will be 12 monthly repayments of 30,000 ÷ 12 = 2,500, and 12 monthly instalments of interest of 3,000 ÷ 12 = 250. If the loan were to be repaid over 24 months, the management committee might still decide to charge interest of 10 per cent per year. In this case, the total interest on the loan would be 2 x 3,000 = 6,000. Using the straight-line method, there would be 24 monthly repayments of 30,000 ÷ 24 = 1,250 and 24 monthly instalments of interest of 6,000 ÷ 24 = 250.

Loan registers

A **loan register** should be kept for each loan issued. This could simply be a page in an exercise book. The loan register provides an accessible record of the administration of each loan. It saves having to go back through all the transactions in the cash and bank books every time there is a query.

The loan register should record:

- the amount of the loan;
- the repayment plan;
- the interest or administration charge;
- the repayments received.

Loan register

Name of group: Group A: Dressmaking project

Amount advanced: 30,000   **Date of advance:** 15 January 19XX

Interest rate: 10%

Purpose of loan: Purchase of a sewing machine, table, stool and threads.

Repayment terms: 33,000 repayable in twelve equal monthly instalments starting 15 February 19XX.[1]

Repayments received:

Date	Total received	Voucher	Repayment of capital[2]	Interest remaining	Balance	Comments
February 10	2,750	R5	2,500	250	27,500[3]	On time

NOTES:

1   The case study assumes that an administration charge or interest of 10 per cent is charged on each loan. The total of the advance plus interest is repayable in 12 equal monthly instalments. The first instalment is due one month after the loan is advanced.

2   The amount advanced as a loan is known as the capital.

3   30,000 – 2,500 = 27,500

Figure 37: Example of a loan register

Summary of loans outstanding

The bookkeeper should keep a loan register for each loan. Every time a repayment is received, the bookkeeper should enter it in the cash book or bank book *and* in the relevant loan register.

From the individual loan registers the bookkeeper can prepare a summary of the loans outstanding (see figure 38). This summary should be prepared regularly, and presented to the management committee for their attention.

Group	Loans issued	Repayments received	Balance remaining	Comments
	Summary of loans outstanding at 28 February 19XX			
A	30,000	2,500	27,500	On time
B	50,000	4,167	45,833	On time
C	40,000	3,333	36,667	On time
D	50,000	—	50,000	Late[2]
E	45,000	—	45,000	Late[2]
F	30,000	—	30,000	No repayments due until March
Total	245,000	10,000	235,000[1]	

NOTES:
1   The total of the 'balance remaining' column appears on the balance sheet. (See figure 33.)
2   The management committee should contact groups D and E, who are late with their repayments. The committee should consider charging interest on late repayments. For example, let us assume they decide to charge 2 per cent per month. Group D was due to make a payment of 4,583 on 5 February. If this payment is not made until 26 February, Group D will be required to pay an additional 20 days interest at 2% = 4583 x 2% x 20 ÷ 28 (28 days in February) = 65.

Figure 38: Summary of loans outstanding

Bad debts

Some groups may be unable to repay the loans they have received. The management committee should contact the group to find out what the problem is and to try to work out a new repayment plan.

However, when it becomes clear that a loan is unlikely to be recovered, the management committee should instruct the bookkeeper to adjust the accounting records to record the amount that has been lost from the scheme. Accountants describe this as **writing off** the loan.

Loans which cannot be recovered are known as **bad debts**. The bookkeeper should record the details of the write-off in the loan register and on the summary of loans outstanding.

For example, let us assume that the balance outstanding from Group E cannot be recovered. Although the project should continue to chase the debt, the accounting records should be adjusted to reflect the fact that the loan is unlikely to be repaid. The 'write-off' is recorded on the loan register (figure 39) and on the summary of loans outstanding (figure 40).

Loan register

Name of group: Group E

Amount advanced: 45,000   **Date of advance:** 28 January 19XX

Interest rate: 10%

Purpose of loan: Purchase of a grinding mill.

Repayment terms: 49,500 repayable in twelve equal monthly instalments starting 28 February 19XX.

Repayments received:

Date	Total received	Voucher	Repayment of capital	Interest	Balance remaining	Comments
						45,000 written off on 28 February 19XX.

Figure 39: Example of loan register, showing write-off of bad debt

Summary of loans outstanding at 28 February 19XX

Group	Loan issued	Repayments received	Bad debts written off	Balance remaining	Comments
A	30,000	2,500		27,500	On time
B	50,000	4,167		45,833	On time
C	40,000	3,333		36,667	On time
D	50,000	-		50,000	Late
E	45,000	-	45,000	NIL	Written off
F	30,000	-		30,000	No repayment due until March
Total	245,000	10,000	45,000	190,000	

Figure 40: Summary of loans outstanding, showing write-off of bad debt

The bookkeeper should show the write-off as an expense of the scheme on the balance sheet. See figure 41 notes 1 and 3:

Balance Sheet at 28 February 19XX

	Notes	28 February	31 January
Assets			
Cash		54,233	58,500
Bank balance		41,367	51,700
Loans outstanding	1	190,000	215,000
Total Assets		285,600	325,200
Liabilities			
Savings held	2	(139,000)	(133,000)
Net Assets		146,600	192,200
Represented by:			
Grant received		200,000	200,000
Accumulated deficit	3	(53,400)	(7,800)
Net Assets		146,600	192,200

Notes on the calculations:
1 Loans outstanding:

		28 February	31 January
Opening loans outstanding		215,000	–
Add:	Loans issued	30,000	215,000
Less:	Loans repaid (excluding interest)	(10,000)	–
	Loans written off	(45,000)	–
		190,000	215,000

2 Savings held:

		28 February	31 January
Opening savings held		133,000	–
Add:	Savings deposited	9,000	133,00
Less:	Savings repaid	(3,000)	–
		139,000	133,000

3 Accumulated deficit:

		28 February	31 January
Opening deficit		7,800	–
Add:	Administration expenses	1,600	7,800
	Loan written off	45,000	–
Less:	Interest received	(1,000)	–
		53,400	7,800

Figure 41: Balance sheet, showing write-off of bad debt

Minimising bad debts

The management committee should take steps to minimise the non-repayment of loans. Borrowers should understand that future loan applications will not be considered unless the current loan is repaid.

The management committee should monitor all loans closely. If the project is in regular contact with borrowers, problems can be discussed at an early stage. In order to minimise losses resulting from bad debts, the committee could consider doing one or more of the following:

- Building an element of security into the loans. There are various ways of doing this; for example, loans could be guaranteed by a group of the borrower's neighbours. In addition, the project managers could agree (in writing) with the borrower that the equipment purchased with the loan remains the property of the project until the loan is fully repaid. In the case study, if the project could recover the grinding mill from Group E and sell it, the sale proceeds would count as a part repayment of the loan and the amount to be written off would be reduced accordingly.
- Linking credit and savings. The project could require participants to save with the scheme for a certain period before becoming eligible for a loan. Another advantage of a combined credit and savings scheme is that, if borrowers know that their loan has been provided out of the savings of their neighbours, they may feel more obligation to keep their repayments up to date.
- Obtaining references on loan applicants.

Summary of this chapter

1 Applicants for loans should submit a **budget** and **repayment plan** with their loan application.
2 The project should draw up a **loan agreement** for every loan to ensure that both parties (the organisers of the credit scheme and the borrower) understand the terms of the loan.
3 The bookkeeper should keep a **loan register** for each loan to record repayments received and the balance remaining.
4 The bookkeeper should prepare a **summary of loans outstanding** regularly so that the committee members can review the progress of each loan.
5 The committee should contact any groups which are not up to date with their repayments, discuss the problem with them, and agree a new **repayment plan**.
6 A loan which cannot be recovered is a **bad debt**. The bookkeeper should **write off** the debt in the accounting records when instructed to do so by the management committee.

Chapter 7:
Administration of savings

In order to administer the saving scheme efficiently, the bookkeeper should keep a **savings card** for each saver. The savings card should record all transactions with the saver. An example is shown below:

		Saver: 1			
Date	**Voucher**	**Deposited**	**Withdrawn**	**Balance**	**Received by**
Jan 2	BR2[1]	25,000		25,000	Cashier
Feb 1	R1[1]	2,000		27,000	Cashier

NOTE: Saver 1 deposited 25,000 *by cheque* on 2 January (see figure 5) and 2,000 *in cash* on 1 February (see figure 27).

Figure 42: Example of a savings card

Each saver should have a **savings card** or book which is a copy of the card held by the credit and savings scheme. The savings card or book is sometimes called a **passbook**. The saver should bring the card to the cashier when making a deposit or requesting a withdrawal.

A saving scheme operates like a bank for the participants. The savings card is the saver's 'bank statement': it records all the saver's transactions with the scheme.

Deposits

Whenever a saver deposits money, the cashier should issue a receipt voucher and initial both copies of the savings card.

	Receipt voucher		
Credit scheme _____		Voucher number _R7_	
Received from _____*Saver 3*_____	Amount _500_		
Description _____*Deposit*_____			
Received by _*Cashier*_	Date _25 February 19XX_		

Figure 43: Example of a receipt voucher

Withdrawals

Before making a payment to a saver, the cashier should check that the balance on the saver's card is enough to cover the amount requested.

The management committee may decide that savers must give notice in advance when they want to withdraw savings from the scheme.

The cashier should complete a payment voucher and ask the saver to sign the voucher and both copies of the savings card, to acknowledge receipt of the money. Whenever a saver deposits or withdraws money, the cashier should take the opportunity to check that the details on the project's copy of the savings card agree exactly with the saver's copy.

Payment voucher

Credit scheme _____ Voucher number __*000056*__

Paid to __*Saver 4*__ Amount __*3,000*__

Description __*Repaid by cheque*__

Authorised by _*Cashier*_ Received by __*Saver 4*__ Date __*8 February 19XX*__

Figure 44: Example of a payment voucher

Using the cash and bank books for January (figures 14,15,17 and 18) and for February (figures 27 - 30) the savings cards can be completed as shown in figure 45 (overleaf).

Monthly savings summary

In order to produce the balance sheet at the end of the month the bookkeeper will need to calculate the total savings held by the scheme. The bookkeeper should prepare a summary of the savings held at the end of each month:

Savings summary at 28 February 19XX

Saver	Balance held
Saver 1	27,000
Saver 2	46,500
Saver 3	53,500
Saver 4	10,000
Saver 5	2,000
Total	139,000

Figure 46: Monthly savings summary

Saver: 1					
Date	**Voucher**	**Deposited**	**Withdrawn**	**Balance**	**Rec'd by**
Jan 2	BR2	25,000		25,000	Cashier
Feb 1	R1	2,000		27,000	Cashier

Saver: 2					
Date	**Voucher**	**Deposited**	**Withdrawn**	**Balance**	**Rec'd by**
Jan 2	BR3	45,000		45,000	Cashier
Feb 2	R2	1,500		46,500	Cashier

Saver: 3					
Date	**Voucher**	**Deposited**	**Withdrawn**	**Balance**	**Rec'd by**
Jan 10	R2	50,000		50,000	Cashier
Feb 7	R4	3,000		53,000	Cashier
Feb 25	R7	500		53,500	Cashier

Saver: 4					
Date	**Voucher**	**Deposited**	**Withdrawn**	**Balance**	**Rec'd by**
Jan 31	BR4	13,000		13,000	Cashier
Feb 8	000056		3,000	10,000	Saver 4

Saver: 5					
Date	**Voucher**	**Deposited**	**Withdrawn**	**Balance**	**Rec'd by**
Feb 15	R6	2,000		2,000	Cashier

Figure 45: Savings cards for the case study

Interest

In some saving schemes, savers are entitled to receive interest on their savings. For example, the project might be a simple savings scheme, where a group of neighbours have opened a bank account together. In this case, the interest paid to savers will depend on the interest paid by the bank. The participants might decide to share out all the interest received in proportion to the amount deposited by each saver. Or they might decide to keep some of the interest in a central fund to cover costs of the scheme or to fund joint projects.

In a combined credit and savings scheme, the interest paid to savers must always be *less* than the interest paid by borrowers (see Chapter 8: Sustainability). When the interest is due it should be entered on the savings cards and shown on the balance sheet as an expense of the scheme.

For example, let us assume that interest is calculated at 0.5 per cent of the balance held at the end of each month (equivalent to 6 per cent interest over one year). Interest due at the end of January would have been calculated as follows:

	Savings at 31 Jan	Interest at 0.5%
Saver 1	25,000	x 0.005 = 125
Saver 2	45,000	x 0.005 = 225
Saver 3	50,000	x 0.005 = 250
Saver 4	13,000	x 0.005 = 65
Total	133,000	x 0.005 = 665

Interest due at the end of February is calculated as follows:

	Savings at 28 February	Interest at 0.05%
Saver 1	27,125	x 0.005 = 136
Saver 2	46,725	x 0.005 = 234
Saver 3	53,750	x 0.005 = 268
Saver 4	10,065	x 0.005 = 50
Saver 5	2,000	x 0.005 = 10
Total	139,665	x 0.005 = 698

The bookkeeper should enter the interest on the savings cards (figure 47) and show it as an expense on the balance sheet (figure 48, notes 2 and 3).

Saver: 1

Date	Voucher	Deposited	Withdrawn	Balance	Rec'd by
Jan 2	BR2	25,000		25,000	Cashier
Jan 31	Interest	125		25,125	
Feb 1	R2	2,000		27,125	Cashier
Feb 28	Interest	136		27,261	

Saver: 2

Date	Voucher	Deposited	Withdrawn	Balance	Rec'd by
Jan 2	BR3	45,000		45,000	Cashier
Jan 31	Interest	225		45,225	
Feb 2	R3	1,500		46,725	Cashier
Feb 28	Interest	234		46,959	

Saver: 3

Date	Voucher	Deposited	Withdrawn	Balance	Rec'd by
Jan 10	R2	50,000		50,000	Cashier
Jan 31	Interest	250		50,250	
Feb 7	R5	3,000		53,250	Cashier
Feb 25	R8	500		53,750	Cashier
Feb 28	Interest	268		54,018	

Saver: 4

Date	Voucher	Deposited	Withdrawn	Balance	Rec'd by
Jan 31	BR4	13,000		13,000	Cashier
Jan 31	Interest	65		13,065	
Feb 8	000056		3,000	10,065	Saver 4
Feb 28	Interest	50		10,115	

Saver: 5

Date	Voucher	Deposited	Withdrawn	Balance	Rec'd by
Feb 15	R6	2,000		2,000	Cashier
Feb 28	Interest	10		2,010	

Figure 47: Savings cards, showing interest received

Balance Sheet at 28 February 19XX

	Notes	28 February	31 January
Assets			
Cash		54,233	58,500
Bank balance		41,367	51,700
Loans outstanding	1	190,000	215,000
Total Assets		285,600	325,200
Liabilities			
Savings held	2	(140,363)	(133,665)
Net Assets		145,237	191,535
Represented by:			
Grant received		200,000	200,000
Accumulated deficit	3	(54,763)	(8,465)
Net Assets		145,237	191,535

Notes on the calculations:

1 Loans outstanding:

		28 February	31 January
Opening loans outstanding		215,000	–
Add:	Loans issued in February	30,000	215,000
Less:	Loans repaid (excluding interest)	(10,000)	–
	Loans written off	(45,000)	–
		190,000	215,000

2 Savings held:

		28 February	31 January
Opening savings held		133,665	–
Add:	Savings deposited in February	9,000	133,000
	Interest credited	698	665
Less:	Savings repaid in February	(3,000)	–
		140,363	133,665

Savings summary:

Saver	Balance held per savings card	
	28 February	31 January
Saver 1	27,261	25,125
Saver 2	46,959	45,225
Saver 3	54,018	50,250
Saver 4	10,115	13,065
Saver 5	2,010	—
Total	140,363	133,665

3 Accumulated deficit:

		28 February	31 January
Opening deficit		8,465	–
Add:	Administration expenses	1,600	7,800
	Interest paid	698	665
	Loan written off	45,000	–
Less:	Interest received	(1,000)	–
		54,763	8,465

Figure 48: Balance sheet, showing interest paid to savers

A summary of this chapter

1 The bookkeeper should prepare a **savings card** for each saver, to be kept by the project. The bookkeeper should record all transactions with the saver on the savings card.

2 Each saver should also be given their own **savings card**, with a record of the details of their transactions with the saving scheme.

3 The cashier should issue a **receipt voucher** whenever a saver deposits money. The cashier should sign the receipt voucher to confirm that she or he has received the money.

4 The cashier should use a **payment voucher** whenever a saver withdraws savings from the scheme. The saver should sign the payment voucher to confirm that he or she has received the money.

5 Whenever a saver makes a deposit or a withdrawal, the cashier and the saver should check that the two copies of the **savings card** (the scheme's copy and the saver's copy) match exactly.

6 The bookkeeper should enter **interest** due on each savings card and add it to the balance held. The bookkeeper should enter the interest on the saver's copy of the card when the saver next makes a deposit or withdrawal.

7 **Interest** is an expense of the savings scheme and is added to the accumulated deficit on the balance sheet (or deducted from an accumulated surplus).

CHAPTER 8: SUSTAINABILITY

Combined credit and savings schemes

The case study used throughout this book describes a combined credit and savings scheme. In a combined scheme, savers' deposits are used to make loans to borrowers. Usually, interest is charged on loans to borrowers, and interest is paid to savers for the use of their money.

For the scheme to continue to operate, the interest charged to borrowers will need to be enough to cover the expenses of the scheme. We have seen that the expenses of a credit and saving scheme fall into three main categories:

- administration expenses;
- bad debts written-off;
- interest paid to savers.

If the interest received from borrowers during an accounting period is greater than the total expenses incurred during that accounting period, the scheme has made a **surplus** for that period. If the interest received is less than the total expenses there is a **deficit** for that accounting period.

In our case study, the balance sheet in figure 48 shows a deficit for February of 46,298 and an accumulated deficit at 28 February of 54,763. This is not a **sustainable** situation. If the deficit continues to increase, the scheme will fail because it will not be able to repay savers.

Revolving loan funds

Sustainability is also an important issue for credit schemes which are not linked to savings schemes. Many credit schemes are set up with a grant from a donor. Loans are made from the original grant and, when these are repaid, further loans are made to other beneficiaries. Such a scheme is sometimes called a **revolving loan fund** because the idea is that the funds *revolve* and benefit many borrowers in turn.

However, in practice many revolving loan funds fail to revolve. There are three main reasons for such failures. Firstly, the people managing the project may underestimate the importance of maintaining accurate accounting records and keeping track of loan repayments. Participants who are making repayments on time will lose confidence in the project if they see that other groups are not repaying their loans.

Secondly, the interest charged on loans may not be enough to cover the expenses of the scheme: the administration costs and bad debts.

Thirdly, the interest charged may not be enough to maintain the value of the revolving fund, because of an increase in prices, or inflation.

Inflation

An increase in the general level of prices in an economy is called **inflation**. If the interest charged on loans is less than the rate of inflation, borrowers are not repaying enough to enable the fund to revolve.

In our case study the credit scheme received a grant of 200,000 on 1 January. Let us suppose that on 1 January this was enough to purchase 5 millet mills at 40,000 each. Economists call this the **purchasing power** of the fund. If prices are rising at 5 per cent per year, millet mills will cost 42,000 each by 31 December. Therefore, unless the fund has received interest of at least 10,000 (5 per cent of 200,000) during the year, the purchasing power of the fund will have fallen, and there will not be enough money to buy 5 new millet mills.

If a borrower borrows 40,000 on 1 January he or she has enough to purchase one millet mill. If the borrower repays 40,000 by 31 December, this will not be enough for a new borrower to purchase a millet mill, because they now cost 42,000.

In a situation of high or unpredictable inflation it will be difficult to calculate the appropriate interest rate to charge borrowers in order to sustain the purchasing power of the revolving fund. In such a situation it would be sensible to link the loan repayments to a hard currency, such as US dollars.

For example, consider the loan to Group C in the case study: 44,000 repayable over 12 months from 28 February. Let us assume that the exchange rate between the currency of the case study country and the US dollar is as follows:

January 19XX	$1 = 100
February 19XX	$1 = 130
March 19XX	$1 = 140

The value of the loan (plus interest of 10 per cent) issued in January in dollars was $440 (44,000 ÷ 100). This means that the twelve monthly instalments for repayment would be equivalent to $37 ($440 ÷ 12 rounded to nearest $). Therefore, if the loan repayments are linked to the US dollar, the borrower should repay 37 x 130 = 4,810 on 28 February and 37 x 140 = 5,180 on 28 March.

Sustainability and accessibility

A sustainable revolving credit scheme is an attractive prospect for donors: their original donation will be re-cycled to reach many beneficiaries.

For a loan fund to be sustainable without further injections of funds from donors, we have seen that the interest charged on loans will need to be high enough to cover the revenue expenses of the fund (administration costs, bad debts, interest paid to savers) and inflation.

The required interest rate may be more than the beneficiaries can afford to pay. However, sustainability may not be the primary objective of the credit scheme. The management committee may decide that being able to offer low interest rates is more important.

Donors may be willing to fund some of the revenue expenses of a credit scheme in order to make the loans cheaper (by charging less interest) and therefore more accessible.

A donor might specify that part of their grant could be used to fund revenue expenses. For example, in the case study, the project received a grant of 200,000. If we assume that 60,000 was given to fund revenue expenses, we can amend the balance sheet in figure 48 as follows:

Balance Sheet at 28 February 19XX			
	Notes	**28 February**	**31 January**
Assets			
Cash		54,233	58,500
Bank balance		41,367	51,700
Loans outstanding		190,000	215,000
Total Assets		285,600	325,200
Liabilities			
Savings held		(140,363)	(133,665)
Net Assets		145,237	191,535
Represented by:			
Grant received		140,000	140,000
Accumulated surplus	1	5,237	51,535
Net Assets		145,237	191,535
Note:			
1 Surplus:			
Surplus brought forward		51,535	—
Grant received		—	60,000
Administration expenses		(1,600)	(7,800)
Interest paid		(698)	(665)
Loan written off		(45,000)	—
Interest received		1,000	—
Surplus carried forward		5,237	51,535

Figure 49: Balance sheet, showing grant received for revenue expenses

A summary of this chapter

1 The sustainability of a credit and savings scheme depends on:
   - the maintenance of accurate accounting records
   - charging an interest rate on loans that is enough to cover the administration expenses of the scheme, bad debts, interest paid to savers and inflation.
2 Sustainability may not be the primary objective of the scheme. The management committee of a credit scheme may decide to subsidise the loans by reducing the rate of interest charged to make them more affordable.

Chapter 9: Stock

Instead of making loans, some credit schemes provide goods on credit to participants. For example, an animal traction project may receive a grant which it uses to purchase ox-ploughs and bean seeds. It then sells the ploughs and seeds to local groups. Some groups are able to pay for their ploughs or seeds immediately. Others are allowed to pay later: they receive their ploughs and seeds **on credit**.

Items which a project holds for resale are known as **stock**. Once a project is handling stock the project leaders should consider the following aspects of stock management:

- record keeping;
- security;
- the value of the stock;
- the condition and useful life of the stock (particularly if the goods held in stock are perishable).

The management committee should appoint a **storekeeper** to handle stock movements and record keeping. If the project is small the book keeper may also be responsible for the stock.

Security

The storekeeper should ensure that there is a secure place in which to keep the stock. The project may have to rent a warehouse or compound, but for small items a lockable room or cupboard may be sufficient.

The store should be organised so that there is a separate location for each stock item. For example, there might be one shelf for tins of bean seeds and another shelf for tins of melon seeds. Only one person should have access to the store. A member of the management committee should hold the spare keys in a sealed, signed envelope (as described for the spare key to the cash box, in Chapter 2 under Cash handling).

Record keeping

The storekeeper should keep the following records:

- stock cards;

- a stock issue book;
- a loan register for each group which has received items on credit.

Stock cards

A separate **stock card** should be maintained by the storekeeper for each category of stock. For example, in the animal traction project above, there are two types of stock: ploughs and bean seeds. The storekeeper would need two stock cards, one for ploughs and one for tins of bean seeds.

The record keeping for stock is similar to that for cash. The stock card records all movements of stock - stock received into the store and stock issued.

Stock Card					
Date	**Details Issued to/ received from**	**Cost**		**Quantity**	
		Movement	Balance	Movement	Balance

Figure 50: Layout of a stock card

Stock received

Whenever items arrive in the store the storekeeper should record the following details on the appropriate stock card (see figure 51):

- the date the goods were received into the store;
- the name of the person supplying the goods;
- the price paid (in the 'cost movement' column);
- the quantity received (in the 'quantity movement' column);

The storekeeper should update the 'balance' columns by:

- adding the price paid for this delivery to the amount in the 'cost balance' column;
- adding the number of units received to the 'quantity balance'.

The price paid for transporting goods to the store is part of the cost of those goods and should be entered on the stock card in the 'cost movement' column.

At any time the storekeeper can calculate the **average cost** of the units in stock by taking the total cost (from the 'cost balance' column) and dividing by the balance in the quantity column. The average cost is used to calculate the cost of stock issued.

Average cost of units of stock	=	Cumulative cost (from stock card)	÷	Quantity (from stock card)

For example, in figure 51, the average cost of ploughs in stock at 26 November is $10,215 \div 100 = 102.15$.

Stock Card: ploughs

Date	Details Issued to/ received from	Cost		Quantity	
		Movement	Balance	Movement	Balance
2.11	Purchase	8,000	8,000	80	80
3.11	Transport	80	8,080	—	80
4.11	Return 2 ploughs	(200)[1]	7,880	(2)[1]	78
25.11	Purchase	2,310	10,190	22	100
26.11	Transport	25	10,215	—	100

NOTE:

1 Issues *from* the store are shown in brackets. For example, on 4 November two ploughs are found to be defective, and are returned to the supplier.

Figure 51: Stock card, showing purchase of stock

Stock issued

Whenever items are issued from the store the storekeeper should record the details in the **stock issue book:**

Stock issue book						
Date	Stock issued	Issued to	Reference[1]	Cost of stock sold	Sales value	Received by

NOTE:

1 Cross-reference to cash book receipts or loan register (for items issued on credit).

Figure 52: Layout of a stock issue book

The stock issue book should record:

- the date the goods were issued from the store;
- the name of the person or group receiving the goods;
- the quantity issued;
- the cost of the stock issued;
- the signature of the person receiving the goods.

Cost of stock issued	=	Average unit cost (from stock card)	X	Quantity issued

Selling price of stock issued	=	Price per unit (as set by project managers)	X	Quantity issued

The storekeeper should also update the stock cards for stock issued. She or he should enter the following details on the appropriate stock card:

- the date the goods were issued from the store;
- the name of the person or group receiving the goods;
- the cost of the stock issued (in the 'cost movement' column);
- the quantity issued (in the 'quantity movement' column);

The storekeeper should update the 'balance' columns by:

- deducting the cost of the stock issued from the amount in the 'cost balance' column;
- deducting the number of units from the 'quantity balance'.

For example, in figure 53, the cost of the two ploughs issued to Village X on 28 November is $(10,215 \div 100) \times 2 = 204$ (rounded to nearest unit). Therefore, the new 'cost balance' is $10,215 - 204 = 10,011$. The new 'quantity balance' is $100 - 2 = 98$.

Stock Card: ploughs

Date	Details Issued to/ received from	Cost		Quantity	
		Movement	Balance	Movement	Balance
2.11	Purchase	8,000	8,000	80	80
3.11	Transport	80	8,080	-	80
4.11	Return 2 ploughs	(200)	7,880	(2)	78
25.11	Purchase	2,310	10,190	22	100
26.11	Transport	25	10,215	-	100
28.11	To Village X	(204)	10,011	(2)	98

Figure 53: Stock card, showing issue of stock

Items issued on credit

Items issued on credit are effectively loans. Those who have received items on credit and have not yet repaid what they owe are **debtors** of the project in the same way as those who have received loans.

The terms of the credit must be clear to the recipients. The individuals or groups who receive items on credit must understand when repayments are due. The management committee must monitor closely the level of outstanding credit.

Record keeping is similar to that for loans of cash. The bookkeeper should open a loan register for each individual or group which receives items on credit. The loan register should record the items taken on credit, the repayments made, and the balance outstanding (see figure 54).

Loan register						
Name of group: Village Y						
Date	Reference	Stock issued	Value	Repaid	Balance	Received by
28.11	LR1	3 ploughs	345		345	Village Y

Figure 54: Loan register for stock issued on credit

If the project is dealing with only a small number of groups, the bookkeeper might find it easier to record all the credit sales and repayments on one loan register with a separate column for each debtor (see figure 58).

The bookkeeper could combine the loan register with the stock issue book (as shown in figure 59) if preferred.

In order to illustrate these principles we will use a second case study. Let us assume that an animal traction project starts on 1 November and that the transactions for November were as listed below. (There is no bank account.)

1 November	Grant received from donor: 14,000
1 November	Warehouse rent paid: 1,000
1 November	Purchase stationery: 500
2 November	Purchase 80 ploughs @ 100 each: 8,000
2 November	Purchase 60 tins bean seeds: 3,000
3 November	Transport ploughs to project store: 80
3 November	Purchase lock for warehouse: 100

4 November	Return 2 defective ploughs to supplier. Received refund of 200
25 November	Purchase 22 ploughs @ 105 each: 2,310
26 November	Transport of ploughs to project store: 25
28 November	Village X pays cash for 2 ploughs (115 each) and 5 tins bean seeds (65 per tin)
28 November	3 ploughs sold on credit to Village Y for 115 each
28 November	Village Y pays cash for 5 tins bean seeds (65 per tin)
30 November	1 plough sold on credit to Village Z for 115

These transactions entered in the cash book, stock issue book, debtors' ledger, and stock cards are shown in figures 55 to 60.

(Readers could test their understanding of record keeping for stock by practising writing up these records themselves using the blank forms in Appendix 3 at the end of the book.)

Cash book: receipts								
Date	Description	Voucher	Amount	Grant	Stock	Cash sales	Loans repaid	Other
1.11	Grant from donor	R1	14,000	14,000				
2.11	Refund re ploughs	R2	200		200			
28.11	From Village X	R3	555			555		
28.11	From Village Y	R4	325			325		
Total			15,080	14,000	200	880		

Figure 55: Animal traction project cash book: receipts

Cash book: payments						
Date	Description	Voucher	Amount	Stock	Admin	Other
1.11	Rent warehouse	1	1,000		1,000	
1.11	Buy stationery	2	500		500	
2.11	Buy 80 ploughs	3	8,000	8,000		
2.11	Buy 60 tins bean seeds	4	3,000	3,000		
3.11	Transport ploughs	5	80	80		
3.11	Buy lock for warehouse	6	100		100	
25.11	Buy 22 ploughs	7	2,310	2,310		
26.11	Transport ploughs	8	25	25		
30.11	Carried forward	–	65			65
Total			15,080	13,415	1,600	65

NOTE: The cost of transporting the ploughs to the project store is included as part of the cost of the stock *not* as an administration expense.

Figure 56: Animal traction project cash book: payments

Stock issue book

Date	Stock issued	Issued to	Reference	Cost of stock sold	Sales value	Rec'd by
28.11	2 ploughs	Village X	R3	204	230	
28.11	5 tins bean seeds	Village X	R3	250	325	
28.11	3 ploughs	Village Y	LR1	306	345	
28.11	5 tins bean seeds	Village Y	R4	250	325	
30.11	1 plough	Village Z	LR2	102	115	
Total				1,112	1,340	

Figure 57: Animal traction project: stock issue book

Loan register

Date	Details	Reference	Stock issued/ (repayments made)	Village Y	Village Z
28.11	Village Y 3 ploughs	LR1	345	345	
30.11	Village Z 1 plough	LR2	115		115
Total			460	345	115

Figure 58: Animal traction project: loan register

Stock issue book and loan register

Date	Details	Cost of stock issued	Reference	Sales value/ (repayments made)	Village X	Village Y	Village Z
28.11	Village X 2 ploughs	204	R3	230	230		
28.11	Village X 5 tins	250	R3	325	325		
28.11	Village X payment		R3	(555)	(555)		
28.11	Village Y 3 ploughs	306	LR1	345		345	
28.11	Village Y 5 tins	250	R4	325		325	
30.11	Village Y payment		R4	(325)		(325)	
30.11	Village Z 1 plough	102	LR2	115			115
Total		1,112		460	—	345	115

Figure 59: Animal traction project: combined stock issue book and loan register

Stock Card: tins of bean seeds

Date	Details Issued to/ received from	Cost		Quantity	
		Movement	Balance	Movement	Balance
2.11	Buy 60 tins	3,000	3,000	60	60
28.11	To Village X	(250)[1]	2,750	(5)	55
28.11	To Village Y	(250)[2]	2,500	(5)	50

NOTES:
1 (3,000 ÷ 60) x 5 = 250
2 (2,750 ÷ 55) x 5 = 250

Stock Card: ploughs

Date	Details Issued to/ received from	Cost		Quantity	
		Movement	Balance	Movement	Balance
2.11	Purchase	8,000	8,000	80	80
3.11	Transport	80[1]	8,080	-	80
4.11	Return 2 ploughs	(200)	7,880	(2)	78
25.11	Purchase	2,310	10,190	22	100
26.11	Transport	25[1]	10,215	–	100
28.11	To Village X	(204)[2]	10,011	(2)	98
28.11	To Village Y	(306)[2]	9,705	(3)	95
30.11	To Village Z	(102)	9,603	(1)	94

Notes on the calculations:
1 The cost of transporting the ploughs to the project store is added to the cost of stock.
2 Average cost of ploughs at 26 November:
    10,215 ÷ 100 = 102 (rounded to nearest unit)
    Therefore, 2 ploughs @ 102 = 204
    3 ploughs @ 102 = 306

Figure 60: Animal traction project: stock cards for bean seeds and ploughs

Using the information from the cash book, debtors' ledger, and stock cards we can produce the balance sheet at 30 November:

Animal traction project
Balance sheet at 30 November 19XX

	Notes	
Cash		65
Stock	1	12,103
Debtors	2	460
		12,628
Grant received		14,000
Deficit	3	(1,372)
		12,628

Notes:

1 Stock

Ploughs	9,603
Tins of bean seeds	2,500
Total	12,103

2 Debtors: see loan register.

3 Deficit

Sales (from stock issue book)	1,340
Cost of stock sold[a]	(1,112)
Gross profit	228
Administration expenses	(1,600)
Deficit[b]	(1,372)

NOTES:

a. The cost of stock sold figure is taken from the stock issue book. It can be checked using the following reconciliation:

Stock brought forward	—	
Stock purchased (13,415 – 200)		13,215
Less: Stock carried forward		(12,103)
Cost of stock sold		1,112

b. The calculation of the surplus generated or deficit incurred by a commercial organisation for a particular accounting period is called the profit and loss account.

Figure 61: Animal traction project: balance sheet

Checking the stock

From time to time the management committee should check that amounts shown in the stock records agree to the stock actually held in the store.

The committee member(s) should count the stock item by item, record the quantity counted, and compare this total to the balance on the stock cards. Any differences should be investigated with the storekeeper. This procedure is called a **stocktake**. The stocktake could be recorded as follows:

Stock item	Quantity counted	Quantity per stock card	Difference (if any)	Comments
Ploughs	94	94		4 ploughs broken
Tins of bean seeds	49	50	1	

Figure 62: Example of stocktake record

If the missing item cannot be found, the stock card should be adjusted to record the actual stock held:

		Stock Card: tins of bean seeds			
Date	Details Issued to/ received from	**Cost**		**Quantity**	
		Movement	Balance	Movement	Balance
2.11	Buy 60 tins	3,000	3,000	60	60
28.11	To Village X	(250)	2,750	(5)	55
28.11	To Village Y	(250)	2,500	(5)	50
30.11	Stock take write-off	(50)[1]	2,450	(1)	49

NOTE

1 Cost of 1 tin written-off: 2,500 ÷ 50 = 50. This amount will appear as an expense in the Balance Sheet (see figure 65).

Figure 63: Stock card, showing stocktake write-off

The value of the stock

We have seen that stock is recorded in the accounting records at **average cost**. For example, the value of the 94 ploughs in stock at 30 November (from figure 60) is 9,603. This is made up of:

78 ploughs purchased for 7,880 including transport	7,880
22 ploughs purchased for 2,335 including transport	2,335
Less: 6 ploughs issued at 102 each	(612)
Value of ploughs held at 30 November 19XX	9,603

The average cost of each plough is 9,603 ÷ 94 = 102. The ploughs are currently being sold for 115 each. However, the stock take (figure 62) has revealed that 4 of the ploughs are broken. It is likely that the broken ploughs are now worth *less* than the average cost of 102 each. The accounting records should be adjusted to reflect this.

If we assume that the broken ploughs are now worth nothing, we can update the stock card as follows:

Date	Details Issued to/ received from	Cost Movement	Cost Balance	Quantity Movement	Quantity Balance
		Stock Card: ploughs			
2.11	Purchase	8,000	8,000	80	80
3.11	Transport	80	8,080	–	80
4.11	Return 2 ploughs	(200)	7,880	(2)	78
25.11	Purchase	2,310	10,190	22	100
26.11	Transport	25	10,215	–	100
28.11	To Village X	(204)	10,011	(2)	98
28.11	To Village Y	(306)	9,705	(3)	95
30.11	To Village Z	(102)	9,603	(1)	94
30.11	Write-off of damaged stock	(408)[1]	9,195	(4)	90

NOTE: 1 Cost of 4 ploughs written-off: (9,603 ÷ 94) x 4 = 408. This amount will appear as an expense in the Balance Sheet (see figure 65).

Figure 64: Animal traction project: stock card, showing write-off of damaged stock

Balance sheet at 30 November 19XX - Amended

	Notes	
Cash		65
Stock	1	11,645
Debtors	2	460
		12,170
Grant received		14,000
Deficit	3	(1,830)
		12,170

Notes:

1 Stock

Ploughs	9,195
Tins of bean seeds	2,450
Total	11,645

2 Debtors: see loan register.

3 Deficit

Sales (from stock issue book)	1,340
Cost of stock sold	(1,112)
Gross profit	228
Administration expenses	(1,600)
Stock write-offs (50 + 408)	(458)
Deficit	(1,830)

Figure 65: Animal traction project: amended balance sheet, showing stock write-offs

A summary of this chapter

1 The management committee should appoint a **storekeeper** to be responsible for the record keeping and security of the stock.

2 The storekeeper should keep the following records:

- a **stock card** for each type of stock;
- a **stock issue book** to record all stock going out;
- a **loan register** to record items issued on credit and repayments received.

3 From time to time the management committee should check the stock system by carrying out a **stocktake**.

CHAPTER 10:
CHECKING THE ACCOUNTS

We have seen that checking should go on throughout the accounting process. For example, the actual cash in the cash box is counted to see if the total agrees with the total recorded in the cash book; the bank statement is reconciled to the bank book. However, from time to time, usually every year, the management committee should organise a check which is independent of the accounts staff.

An independent examination of and expression of opinion on the books and records of an organisation is called an **audit.** The management committee should appoint an experienced accountant from outside the project to conduct the audit. Donors may appoint their own auditor or may even send one of their own staff to conduct the audit.

An audit need not be a difficult process if the project knows what to expect. The auditor may be able to make helpful recommendations to simplify or streamline the accounting system. Experienced accountants are used to having their work checked, and approach audits as a learning opportunity.

What the auditor will be looking for

The auditor will usually start with the latest balance sheet and will be trying to establish whether it gives a **true and fair view** of the financial position of the organisation. The auditor will be looking for **evidence** that the amounts shown on the balance sheet are accurate.

For example, consider the balance sheets shown figures 41, 48, 61 and 65. The auditor should consider each item in turn, asking questions and carrying out tests. For example,

- Is the cash figure accurate?
  Test: Count the cash and check the total against the total shown in the balance sheet.
- Is the 'cash at bank' figure accurate?
  Test: Obtain the latest bank statement and check the bank reconciliation.

- Is the stock figure accurate?
  Tests: 1 Prepare a summary of stock held from the stock cards and check the total against the total shown on the balance sheet.
  2 Carry out a stocktake.
- Is the figure for credit outstanding accurate?
  Tests: 1 Compare the loans summary with the figure shown on the balance sheet.
  2 Select a sample of borrowers, ask them how much they think they owe to the project, and compare their answers with the figures on the loans register.
  3 Check that loan agreements exist and that the repayments are up to date.
- Is the figure for 'savings held' correct?
  Tests: 1 Check that the figure shown on the balance sheet is the same as the total on the savings summary.
  2 Select a sample of savers:
    - check the saving summary against the savings cards;
    - contact the savers and check that their savings cards agree with the project's copy of the card.

The auditor should also investigate whether the internal controls are adequate. For example, the auditor should check:

- Who has keys to the cash box, safe and store?
- Where are the unused cheques and receipt vouchers kept?
- Who can sign the cheques?
- What cash payments can the cashier make without prior authorisation from the treasurer?

The auditor should present a **report** of his or her findings and recommendations to the management committee of the project.

A summary of this chapter

1 The management committee should organise an annual **audit** of the accounting records.
2 The auditor should present a **report** of his/her conclusions and recommendations to the management committee.

CHAPTER 11: TEN BASIC PRINCIPLES

1 The management committee should draw up and approve the budget of the scheme before any expenditure takes place.

2 Only the cashier should have access to the cash and only the storekeeper should have access to the store. Spare keys to the cash box and the store should be kept in sealed envelopes held by a member of the management committee.

3 The cashier should regularly count the cash and record the cash count. Each month the treasurer should review the cash count and initial the cash count sheet.

4 Every month the bookkeeper should prepare a bank reconciliation which should be checked by the treasurer.

5 The cashier should record all transactions promptly in the cash or bank book to avoid forgetting to enter anything.

6 The cashier should issue a receipt voucher whenever income is received and use a payment voucher for every payment made.

7 Every month the bookkeeper should prepare a receipts and payments report, a budget and actual report, and a balance sheet, for review by the management committee.

8 For every loan there should be a loan agreement, and the bookkeeper should maintain a loan register.

9 Every saver should have a savings card and the bookkeeper should maintain a matching savings card.

10 The storekeeper should keep a separate stock card for each stock item. From time to time a member of the management committee should check that the physical stock agrees to the stock records (a stocktake).

You may (through self-conceit), having well understood the former instructions, suppose that you are able to manage the Booking of all Trafficking affaires, and so leave your study. You would be wrong. Practise, practise, practise!

Richard Dafforne, 1635 — *The Merchant's Mirrour*

68

GLOSSARY

Accounting period	The period of time covered by a financial report.
Administration charge	A charge for borrowing money. See also 'interest': in some cultures it is not appropriate to use the term 'interest' for such a charge.
Analysed cash book	A cash book with separate columns to record major categories of income and expenditure.
Assets	The things owned by an individual or organisation. For example, cash, money in a bank account, or furniture.
Audit	An independent examination of and expression of opinion on the books and records of an enterprise.
Bad debt	A loan which cannot be recovered.
Balance	1 An amount remaining. For example, the cash balance is the cash remaining in a cash box; the balance of a loan is the amount of the loan less repayments already made. 2 The bookkeeper balances the accounts by agreeing the closing balance in the cash book to the cash held in the cash box (the cash count) and by agreeing the closing balance in the bank book to the bank statement (the bank reconciliation).
Balance brought forward	See 'opening balance'.
Balance carried forward	See 'closing balance'.

Balance Sheet	A list of the assets and liabilities of an organisation.
Bank book	The record of the transactions of an organisation with its bank.
Bank Statement	A report issued by the bank (usually monthly) detailing its transactions on behalf of a customer.
Bank reconciliation	An investigation of the difference (if any) between the bank balance shown in the bank book and the bank balance shown on the bank statement.
Bookkeeper	The person responsible for maintaining accounting records.
Budget	An estimate of the likely income and expenditure of an organisation for a specified time period. A costed plan.
Budget and actual report	A comparison of budgeted income and expenditure against actual income and expenditure for an accounting period.
Capital	1 The original funding of a project or organisation. 2 Money advanced as a loan.
Capital expenditure	Expenditure on assets such as equipment, furniture or vehicles.
Cash book	The record of the cash transactions of an organisation. Records all cash coming in and going out.
Cash box	A lockable box in which cash is kept.
Cash count	Counting cash, usually to ensure the amount held agrees with the balance shown in the cash book.

Cashier	The person responsible for cash handling.
Creditor	A person or group who is entitled to receive money from an organisation.
Closing balance	The amount remaining at the end of an accounting period. For example, the closing balance in a cash book is the cash remaining at the end of the accounting period. The closing balance at the end of one accounting period will be the opening balance at the start of the next accounting period.
Debtor	A person or group who owes money to an organisation.
Deficit	If expenditure is greater than income in an accounting period the organisation has incurred a deficit in that accounting period.
Division of duties	Arranging the accounting tasks so that no one person is responsible for all the procedures.
Inflation	A measure of the increase in the general level of prices.
Interest	1 A charge for borrowing money. 2 A payment for lending money. (Usually calculated as a percentage of the amount advanced.)
Invoice	A bill issued by a supplier to a customer.
Liabilities	Amounts owed by an individual or organisation to another individual or organisation. For example, a loan taken but not yet repaid or goods received but not yet paid for.
Loan agreement	An agreement between a lender and a borrower concerning the terms of the loan. For example, the amount, the purpose of the loan, the repayment schedule, and the interest to be charged.

Loan register	A record of the transactions relating to a loan, that is, details of the borrower, the amount advanced, the purpose of the loan, the repayment terms, the interest charged, and the repayments made.
Management committee	The group of people responsible for managing a project. (In this book, used to refer to the people running a credit and savings scheme.)
Management information	Financial summaries and reports prepared for the managers of an organisation.
Net assets	The total assets of an organisation when the total liabilities have been paid. (Sometimes referred to as the 'book value' of the organisation.)
Opening balance	The amount held at the start of an accounting period. For example, the opening balance in the cash book is the cash held at the start of the accounting period. The opening balance at the start of an accounting period should be the same as the closing balance at the end of the previous accounting period.
Passbook	A saver's record of his or her transactions with the saving scheme or a customer's record of his or her transactions with their bank.
Payment voucher	An internal document used to record the details of a payment.
Profit and loss account	A schedule explaining how the surplus generated or deficit incurred by a commercial organisation was achieved.
Receipts and payments report	A summary of the income received and payments made during an accounting period.
Receipt voucher	Document issued by someone receiving money to the person from whom they receive it.

Repayment plan	A plan for the timing and size of instalments to repay a loan.
Revenue expenditure	Expenditure on running costs such as rent, salaries, or fuel.
Savings card	A saver's record of his or her transactions with the saving scheme. The savings card should record all amounts deposited and amounts withdrawn, and any interest paid to the saver.
Stock	Items purchased for resale.
Stocktake	Checking the stock held in the store against the stock records.
Surplus	If income is greater than expenditure in an accounting period the organisation has generated a surplus in that accounting period.
Treasurer	The member of the management committee responsible for overseeing the financial management of the project.
Variance	The difference between the budgeted amount of an item of income or expenditure in an accounting period and the actual amount.
Write-off	An adjustment made in the accounts to reflect a reduction in the value of, or loss of, an asset.

FURTHER READING

Arrosi, S et al (1994) *Funding Community Initiatives*, UNDP/Earthscan.

Bakhoum, I et al (1989) *Banking the Unbankable: Bringing Credit to the Poor*, Panos.

Cammack, J (1992) *Basic Accounting for Small Groups*, Oxfam, Oxford.

Conroy, J D, Taylor, K W, Thapa, G B (1995) *Best Practice of Banking with the Poor*, Foundation for Development Co-operation., Brisbane, Australia.

Devereux, S and Pares H with J Best (1990) *Credit and Savings for Development*, Oxfam, Oxford.

Fall, A (1991) *Cereal Banks at Your Service*, ALIN, Dhakar.

FAO (1989) *Revolving Loan Funds and Credit Programmes for Fishing Communities*, FAO, Rome.

Frimpong-Ansah, J H and Ingham, B (eds) (1992) *Saving for Economic Recovery in Africa*, James Currey.

Hurley, D (1990) *Income Generation Schemes for the Urban Poor*, Oxfam, Oxford.

Lloyd, T and Morrissey, O (eds) (1994) *Poverty, Inequality and Rural Development: Case-Studies in Economic Development, Volume 3*, Macmillan.

Millard, E (1988) *Financial Management of a Small Handicraft Business*, Oxfam, Oxford.

Otero, M and Rhyne, E (1994) *The New World of Micro-enterprise Finance*, Intermediate Technology Publications.

Rogaly, B and Johnson, S (forthcoming, 1997) *Financial Services and Poverty Reduction*, Oxfam, Oxford.

Appendix 1: A worked example

Darfur revolving fund

Information

A farmers' cooperative in Darfur in the west of Sudan are operating a revolving fund selling seeds. The original capital for the fund was a grant from Oxfam of Ls52,500 for the purchase of tomato, melon and cucumber seeds.

A simple accounting system is in operation involving stock cards, a cash book, a bank book, and a stock issue book. The balance sheet of the fund as at 1 January 19XX is attached, together with details of the transactions in January. (All figures are in Sudanese pounds: Ls.) The transactions in January 19XX are as follows:

1.1.XX	Issue of 10 tins of tomato seeds to Kamonga at Ls 500 each.
1.1.XX	Issue of 10 tins of melon seeds to Kawra at Ls 700 each.
2.1.XX	Issue of 8 tins of tomato seeds to Shoba at Ls 500 each.
3.1.XX	Purchase of 13 tins of tomato seeds for Ls 450 each using a cheque.
3.1.XX	Cheque payment of Ls 200, being transport cost of tomato seeds: to be included as part of the cost of the seeds.
4.1.XX	Ls 10,000 received from Kamonga.
5.1.XX	Ls 5,000 received from Shoba.
10.1.XX	Issue of 10 packets of cucumber seeds to Kawra at Ls 100 each.
11.1.XX	Issue of 15 tins of melon seeds to Shoba at Ls 700 each.
12.1.XX	Purchase of 20 tins of melon seeds at Ls 500 each for cash.
15.1.XX	Transfer of Ls 4,000 to the bank.
25.1.XX	It is discovered that Debli village centre can no longer be contacted. The management committee decide to write-off the amount outstanding from Debli.
26.1.XX	Three packets of cucumber seeds are found to be damaged. These will have to be destroyed and written-off on the stock card.
27.1.XX	Stationery for the fund purchased for Ls 1,000 cash.
31.1.XX	Bank statement received. Includes bank charges of Ls 60.

At 1 January 19XX the balance sheet of the fund was as follows:

Balance sheet as at 1 January 19XX
Notes

		Ls
Cash		1,000
Bank		6,500
Stock	1	24,250
Outstandings	2	29,750
		61,500
Capital	3	52,500
Surplus	4	9,000
		61,500

Notes:
1 Stock

		Quantity	Unit cost	Total value	Current selling price
Tomato seeds	1 pound tins	20	400	8,000	500
Melon seeds	1 pound tins	25	500	12,500	700
Cucumber seeds	6 oz packets	50	75	3,750	100
Total				24,250	

2 Debtors

Village	Amount outstanding
Kamonga	6,000
Kawra	6,750
Debli	10,000
Shoba	7,000
Total	29,750

3 Capital: Local purchase in November 19XX by Oxfam:

		Quantity	Unit cost	Total cost
Tomato seeds	1 pound tins	50	400	20,000
Melon seeds	1 pound tins	50	500	25,000
Cucumber seeds	6 oz packets	100	75	7,500
Total				52,500

4 Surplus

Sales	37,500
Cost of stock sold	(28,250)
Gross profit	9,250
Expenses	(250)
Net profit	9,000

Exercises:

1   Write up the stock issue book, cash book, bank book, and stock cards for January 19XX.
2   Prepare a balance sheet with notes as at 31 January 19XX.

Darfur revolving fund: combined stock issue book and loan register

| Stock issued: | | | | | Issued to: | | | |
Date	Details	Ref	Cost of stock sold	Price	Kamonga	Kawra	Debli	Shoba
1 Jan	Debtors brought forward	-		29,750	6,000	6,750	10,000	7,000
1 Jan	10 tins tomato seeds	LR1	4,000	5,000	5,000			
1 Jan	10 tins melon seeds	LR2	5,000	7,000		7,000		
2 Jan	8 tins tomato seeds	LR3	3,200	4,000				4,000
4 Jan	Repayment received	R1		(10,000)	(10,000)			
5 Jan	Repayment received	R2		(5,000)				(5,000)
10 Jan	10 tins cucumber seeds	LR4	750	1,000		1,000		
11 Jan	15 tins melon seeds	LR5	7,500	10,500				10,500
25 Jan	Debt written off	LR6		(10,000)			(10,000)	
			20,450	32,250	1,000	14,750	—	16,500

Darfur revolving fund cash book: receipts

Receipts

Date	Description	Voucher	Amount	From cash	Repayments from villages	Other
1 Jan	Brought forward	—	1,000			1,000
4 Jan	From Kamonga	R1	10,000		10,000	
5 Jan	From Shoba	R2	5,000		5,000	
Total			16,000		15,000	1,000

Darfur revolving fund cash book: payments

Payments

Date	Description	Voucher	Amount	To bank	Stock	Admin	Other
12 Jan	Purchase 20 tins melon seeds	1	10,000		10,000		
15 Jan	Deposit cash at bank	P2	4,000	4,000			
27 Jan	Purchase stationery	P3	1,000			1,000	
31 Jan	Carried forward	—	*1,000*				*1,000*
			16,000	4,000	10,000	1,000	1,000

Darfur revolving fund bank book: receipts

Receipts

Date	Description	Voucher	Amount	From cash	Repayments from villages	Stock	Other
1 Jan	Brought forward	—	6,500				6,500
15 Jan	Cash deposited	BR1	4,000	4,000			
Total			10,500	4,000			6,500

Darfur revolving fund bank book: payments

Payments

Date	Description	Voucher	Amount	To cash	Stock	Admin	Other
3 Jan	Purchase 13 tins tomato seeds	BP1	5,850		5,850		
3 Jan	Delivery of tomato seeds	BP2	200		200		
31 Jan	Bank charges	BP3	60			60	
31 Jan	Carried forward	—	*4,390*				*4,390*
Total			10,500		6,050	60	4,390

Stock cards

Tomato seeds 1 pound tins

Date	Details Issued to/ received from	Cost		Quantity	
		Movement	Balance	Movement	Balance
1.1.XX	Brought forward		8,000		20
1.1.XX	Kamonga	(4,000)	4,000	(10)	10
2.1.XX	Shoba	(3,200)	800	(8)	2
3.1.XX	Purchase	5,850	6,650	13	15
3.1.XX	Transport	200	6,850	—	15

Melon seeds 1 pound tins

Date	Details Issued to/ received from	Cost		Quantity	
		Movement	Balance	Movement	Balance
1.1.XX	Brought forward		12,500		25
1.1.XX	Kawra	(5,000)	7,500	(10)	15
11.1.XX	Shoba	(7,500)	—	(15)	—
12.1.XX	Purchase	10,000	10,000	20	20

Cucumber seeds 6oz packets

Date	Details Issued to/ received from	Cost		Quantity	
		Movement	Balance	Movement	Balance
1.1.XX	Brought forward		3,750		50
10.1.XX	Kawra	(750)	3,000	(10)	40
26.1.XX	Damaged	(225)	2,775	(3)	37

Balance sheet as at 31.1.XX

	Notes	Ls
Cash		1,000
Bank		4,390
Stock	1	19,625
Outstandings	2	32,250
		57,265
Capital		52,500
Surplus	3	4,765
		57,265

Notes:

1 Stock

		Balance Ls
Tomato seeds	1 pound tins	6,850
Melon seeds	1 pound tins	10,000
Cucumber seeds	6 oz packets	2,775
		19,625

2 Debtors

Village	Amount outstanding
Kamonga	1,000
Kawra	14,750
Debli	–
Shoba	16,500
Total	32,250

3 Deficit for January

	Ls	Ls
Sales[a]		27,500
Cost of sales		
Cost of stock sold	20,450	
Damaged stock	225	
		(20,675)
		6,825
Debt written-off		(10,000)
Expenses (1,000 + 60)		(1,060)
		(4,235)
Surplus brought forward		9,000
Deficit Jan XX		(4,235)
Surplus carried forward		4,765

NOTE
a Sales
From stock issue book price column:
5,000 + 7,000 + 4,000 + 1,000 + 10,500 = 27,500

Appendix 2 Blank forms

Bank reconciliation

Balance on bank statement

Less:

Payments in bank book not on statement

    Unpresented cheques

Add:

Income in bank book not yet on statement

Payments on statement not yet in bank book

    Charges   _____

    Balance shown in bank book   _____

Prepared by: (bookkeeper)   Date:

Agreed by: (treasurer)   Date:

Credit scheme loan agreement

Name of group: _____

The credit scheme has agreed to loan you the sum of _____

Interest on this loan will be charged at the rate of_____per annum

The credit scheme agrees that the total amount of the loan, plus

interest, of _____ will be repaid in _____ monthly instalments of

from _____ to _____

The amount loaned by the credit scheme must be used only for the

agreed purpose, namely_____

Interest will be charged on late repayments at the rate of___% per

month.

Signed on behalf of the credit scheme:

Name_____Position_____

Signature_____Date_____

Signed on behalf of the group:

Name_____Position_____

Signature_____Date_____

Cash count sheet

Cash counted

Notes:

_____

Coins:

_____

Total cash counted:

Cash book balance: _____

Difference (if any):   _____

Counted by: (cashier)_____   Date: _____

Agreed by: (treasurer)_____   Date: _____

Credit scheme cash book: receipts

Receipts

Date	Description	Voucher number	Amount	Grants	Loans repaid	Loan interest	Savings	Other
TOTAL								

Credit scheme cash book: payments

Payments

Date	Description	Voucher number	Amount	Loans issued	Savings repaid	Admin. expense	Salaries	Other
	TOTAL							

Loan register

Name of group:

Amount advanced: Date of advance: Interest rate:

Purpose of loan:

Repayment terms:

Repayments received:

Date	Total rec'd	Voucher number	Repayment of capital	Interest	Balance remaining	Comments

Summary of loans outstanding

Group issued	Loan received	Repayments remaining	Balance	Comments
		Total		

Savings card

Saver: 1

Date	Voucher	Deposited	Withdrawn	Balance	Rec'd by

Savings summary at:

Saver	Balance held

Date	Details Issued to/ received from	Cost		Quantity	
		Movement	Balance	Movement	Balance

Stock Card

Date	Stock issued	Issued to	Reference	Cost of stock sold	Sales value	Received by

Stock issue book

INDEX

Other books on financial management and income generation from Oxfam Publications

Basic Accounting for Small Groups

John Cammack

The success of any venture, whatever its size, depends on proper financial control. This book offers a step-by-step guide to basic accounting and financial management techniques. It is written in plain language for people who have no previous experience of accounting and book-keeping. Using simple case studies, the author shows how to construct a budget and a cash-flow forecast, record and control cash payments, draw up an analysed cash book , and a receipts and payments account, operate a bank account, and prepare a budget and actual statement.

John Cammack worked for seven years as the head of Oxfam's Overseas Finance Department. But the procedures that he describes are not specific to Oxfam, or even to development projects. This book should be useful to any small group that needs to keep accurate records of its financial transactions.

ISBN 0 85598 148 2 £5.95

The Financial Management of a Small Handicraft Business

Edward Millard

This short book deals with the basic financial concepts involved in the effective planning of day-to-day operations. It aims to assist small businesses to plan working capital requirements and achieve profitability.

Edward Millard worked for many years as a trainer and marketing manager with Oxfam Trading.

ISBN 0 85598 082 6 £4.95

Income Generation Schemes for the Urban Poor

Donnacadh Hurley

This book examines the reasons for the failure or success of income generation schemes, and stresses the need to be more aware of the harsh economic realities. Special attention is given to the problems faced by poor urban women. The relationship between social and economic development is discussed, and income generation is considered in the context of other strategies for poverty alleviation. The book stresses the need for a market-oriented approach and gives practical advice on developing effective business methods and organisation.

ISBN 0 85598 102 4 £8.95

Women and Economic Policy

Barbara Evers (editor)

This book in the Focus on Gender series is structured around two main themes: macro-economic policy and gender relations; and income-generation projects and empowerment. It contains a series of articles looking at many aspects of women's lives, the effects of economic policies, and how women are adapting and organising to enable their families and communities to survive.

ISBN 0 85598 260 8 £7.95

Gender considerations in Economic Enterprises

Eugenia Piza-Lopez and Candida March (editors)

This account of a 1990 workshop discusses the diverse approaches to working with women on income-generation projects in Asia.

ISBN 0 85598 189 X £4.95

Oxfam Publications

Oxfam (UK and Ireland) publishes a wide range of books, manuals, journals, and resource materials for specialist, academic, and general readers. For a free catalogue, please write to

Oxfam Publishing
274 Banbury Road
Oxford OX2 7DZ, UK

telephone (0)1865 313922
e-mail publish@oxfam.org.uk

Oxfam publications are available from the following agents:
for Canada and the USA: Humanities Press International,
165 First Avenue, Atlantic Highlands, New Jersey
NJ 07716-1289, USA; tel. (908) 872 1441;
fax (908) 872 0717
for southern Africa: David Philip Publishers, PO Box 23408,
Claremont, Cape Town 7735, South Africa; tel. (021) 64 4136;
fax (021) 64 3358.